GIRLS
& YOUNG WOMEN
Inventing

TWENTY TRUE STORIES
ABOUT INVENTORS
PLUS HOW YOU CAN
BE ONE YOURSELF

Frances A. Karnes, Ph.D.
and Suzanne M. Bean, Ph.D.

Edited by Rosemary Wallner

Free Spirit®
PUBLISHING

Library of Congress Cataloging-in-Publication Data
Karnes, Frances A.
    Girls and young women inventing : 20 true stories about inventors plus how you can be one yourself / Frances A. Karnes and Suzanne M. Bean : edited by Rosemary Wallner.
        p.   cm.
    Includes bibliographical references and index.
    Summary: Examines twenty young female inventors and their creations, from Jennifer Donabar and her electric lock to Jeanie Low and her kiddie stool.
        ISBN 0-915793-89-X (alk. pbk.)
    1. Women inventors—United States—Biography—Juvenile literature.
2. Children as inventors—United States—Biography—Juvenile literature.
3. Inventions—United States—History—Juvenile literature. [1. Children as inventors. 2. Inventors. 3. Women—Biography. 4. Inventions—History.]
I. Bean, Suzanne M., 1957–   . II. Wallner, Rosemary, 1964–   . III. Title.
T39.K37   1995
604' .82—dc20   95-16300
                                                                            CIP
                                                                             AC

Cover and book design by MacLean & Tuminelly
Editorial direction by Pamela Espeland
Index prepared by Eileen Quam and Theresa Wolner
10 9 8 7 6 5 4 3 2
Printed in the United States of America

Free Spirit Publishing Inc.
400 First Avenue North, Suite 616
Minneapolis, MN 55401-1730
(612) 338-2068

Dedication

THIS BOOK IS DEDICATED TO FEMALE INVENTORS and to the parents, teachers, and others who have encouraged and supported their creativity.

Acknowledgments

GIRLS AND YOUNG WOMEN ACROSS THE COUNTRY have made this book a reality. The creative and imaginative abilities of these inventors are cause for celebration. The inventors featured here have developed new products or designed significant variations on existing ones. We congratulate them for their accomplishments. We extend our grateful thanks to them and to the other young women with similar creative attributes. All have shared with us the experiences they enjoyed as they tested alternative plans and created new or improved products or processes.

Many people and organizations helped us in our search for young female inventors. Announcements about this project were placed in numerous newsletters, magazines, and journals. Several special interest organizations and trade associations that cater to inventors and report on current and recent inventions assisted with the identification of girls and young women who are making their mark as inventors. Researchers at colleges and universities and personnel employed in research and development departments of business and industrial establishments also shared information with us.

Administrators, colleagues, and staff at our respective universities, The University of Southern Mississippi and The Mississippi University for Women, have continued to support our ideas and work. No one could ask for more positive and supportive environments. There are people at both institutions who assisted with aspects of the book and deserve special recognition. Barbara LeSure and Sherry Honsinger spent many hours preparing the manuscript for presentation to the publisher. Kate Butler Walker gave many helpful suggestions and provided invaluable editing and library research skills. Amanda Reyes assisted with library searches and the bibliography.

A special expression of gratitude is due the adult female inventors who shared their words of motivation and encouragement. Our publisher, Judy Galbraith, has been and will continue to be an outstanding role model and friend. We also want to thank her staff for their able assistance.

Our families continue to be supportive and understanding. To Mark, Meriweather, and Hudson Bean; and to Ray, Christopher, John, Leighanne, and Mary Ryan Karnes, we acknowledge your encouragement and patience, and express our deepest gratitude.

Contents

INTRODUCTION 1
  Inventing Is Fun 1
  About This Book 2

PART ONE: INVENTORS AND THEIR
INVENTIONS 3

CONVENIENCE INVENTIONS 5
  Jennifer Donabar: The Electro-Lock 6
  Jennifer Garcia: The Vacuum Dirt Mat and More 10
  Chelsea Lanmon: The Pocket Diaper and More 14
  Karen Schlangen: The Umbrella Redesigned 19
  Questions to Think About, Ideas to Try 24

WORK-SAVING INVENTIONS 25
  Melissa Jo Buck: The Mop Head Cover and More 26
  Stefanie Lynn Garry: The Adjustable Broom 32
  Katina Stewart: Katina's Clothes Saver 37
  Emma Tillman: The Self-Draining Above-Ground
      Swimming Pool Winter Cover 41
  Jamie Lynn Villella: E. Z. Tools and More 45
  Questions to Think About, Ideas to Try 51

CONSERVATION INVENTIONS 53
  Meghan Renee Hatfield: The Driver's License
      Number Scanner 54
  Jana Kraschnewski: Stalk Board 58
  Questions to Think About, Ideas to Try 64

FUN INVENTIONS 65
  Kellyan Coors: The Tooth Fairy Light, The SHHHH
      Machine, and More 66

Elizabeth Low: Happy Hands 75
Emily Meredith Tucker: Ice Blades 81
Questions to Think About, Ideas to Try 86

HEALTH INVENTIONS 87
Lauren Patricia DeLuca: The Meal Marker 88
Jeri Lee: The Asthmameter and More 93
Laura Neubauer: Neubie's Nebuwhirl 99
Questions to Think About, Ideas to Try 104

SAFETY INVENTIONS 105
Katya Harfmann: Tipper Toes 106
Sarita M. James: Computers and Speech Recognition 111
Jeanie Low: The Kiddie Stool 116
Questions to Think About, Ideas to Try 123

PART TWO: HOW TO BE AN INVENTOR ...125
Get Started 127
Come Up with Ideas 128
Choose an Idea to Pursue 130
Turn Your Idea into an Invention 131
Develop a Sketch 134
Put It All Together 134
Give It a Name 135
Some Information on Patents 137
Marketing Your Invention 138

PART THREE: FOR FURTHER INSPIRATION 141
Female Inventors in History 143
Inspiring Quotations about Inventing and Inventions 146
Organizations and Associations to Contact 151
Books to Read 157

INDEX 162

ABOUT THE AUTHORS 168

Introduction

INVENTING IS FUN

$\mathcal{L}$OOK AROUND YOU. ALMOST EVERYTHING YOU SEE has been invented by someone. You can be an inventor, too. When you think about how to change something to make it easier to use, or think of a new product you might need, you're beginning the invention process.

The girls and young women featured in this book tell their own stories about their inventions. They describe how they came up with their ideas and what inspired them to go forward and make their ideas into working inventions. For many, lack of technical knowledge and money set up barriers and obstacles. But all had goals they wanted to achieve—and all found ways to overcome their problems.

Many of the girls and young women talked with others to find out more information about the inventing process. They found that teachers, parents, and other adults in their communities were helpful and supportive resources. Some of the girls and young women became involved with inventing when their teachers included the study of the invention process in their classes. Many others attended schools that sponsored invention contests, competitions, and fairs. Some participated in local, state, and national invention competitions. Several of them have been granted patents.

ABOUT THIS BOOK

Part One, "Inventors and Their Inventions," includes the stories of girls and young women—all inventors. You'll read about convenience and work-saving inventions, inventions that help to conserve resources, fun inventions, and inventions designed for the health and safety of others. Within each story, you'll learn about the girl or young woman and her invention (or inventions). At the end of each section, you'll find questions that will help you think about the invention process and what you could invent.

Part Two, "How to Be an Inventor," describes the many steps inventors use to turn an idea into a useful, working invention. It includes tips on how to get an idea, and hints on how to name your invention, apply for a patent, and market your invention. You'll also find suggestions on keeping an Inventor's Notebook—a place where you can write down all of your ideas, problems, and solutions.

Part Three, "For Further Inspiration," includes more information to encourage you as you begin the inventing process. You'll read how the number of patents granted to women has been increasing. You'll find a list of female inventors from 3,000 B.C. to the present. In "Inspiring Quotations about Inventing and Inventions," you'll find quotes from women and men about inventions, creativity, and discovery. "Organizations and Associations to Contact" is a listing of places that help people learn about all areas of inventing. Write to these organizations for more information; you'll find that they're helpful and supportive of you and your interests in inventing.

The "Books to Read" section lists several books you may want to read to find out more information. You'll find the books listed under the subheads "Books for Elementary Grades" and "Books for Young Adults and Up." Reading about inventing, inventions, and inventors will help you gain more knowledge. Enjoy these books and learn more about what inspired other inventors.

PART ONE

Inventors and Their Inventions

CONVENIENCE
Inventions

Jennifer Donabar

THE ELECTRO-LOCK

JENNIFER DONABAR was born in 1979 in Milwaukee, Wisconsin. Fifteen years later, she is still living in Milwaukee, where she now attends Solomon Juneau Business High School. Jennifer is an above-average student who is currently on the honor roll. She is involved in volleyball and is a big buddy to two first-graders. Jennifer tries her best on all her assignments and projects.

Jennifer has two caring and considerate parents, Robert and Judy Donabar, whom she loves very much. She also has two older brothers, Brad and Jeff, whom she loves as well. Jennifer has many friends, some of whom are as close to her as her own family.

When Jennifer isn't doing her homework, you might catch her reading, writing, playing volleyball, listening to the radio, or talking to her friends. In addition to being a student, she is employed as a newspaper carrier and a baby-sitter. She hopes to be a successful participant in the business world and maybe travel someday.

LAST YEAR WAS THE FIRST YEAR MY SCHOOL sponsored an Invent America! contest. After a very difficult time trying to come up with an idea for the competition, it finally came to me: an electronic lock.

I always had a tough time opening my locker at school because the lock seemed to stick. I constantly had to ask my friends to open my lock for me. As a result, by the end of the year half of my class knew

*Jennifer
Donabar*

my combination. When inventing my electronic lock, I hoped to make a
lock that was quick, easy, and safe enough to put anywhere. I wanted
people to be able to open the lock by pressing a few buttons. That way,
they wouldn't have to worry about a long combination and wouldn't
have to hassle with a key. The lock would be the solution to a situation
many people consider a common problem. My lock would also be a big
help for people with disabilities.

The first step was to get all of the supplies necessary to construct
my lock including a key pad, electrical wiring, and a distributor. Then
I made a sketch of what my lock would look like; drawing the lock
made the whole inventing procedure a lot easier. After that, I went to
the library and did so much research and investigating on locks and
electrical wiring procedures I thought I would die.

Next, I did all of the mechanical work. I found out which
terminals operated the combinations on the key pad. I hooked up the
distributor, which allowed the lock to open and close. I also hooked up
the battery and wiring. After that, I double-checked my plans and made
sure everything was just right. I finished putting everything together
and in its place, then I closed and sealed the lock. Because I used
electricity to work my lock, I named my invention the "Electro-Lock."

It actually took me a great deal of time to make my lock and complete the rest of the work on the project. My dad was a big help. He helped me with all of the electrical work and the construction of my lock. Both of my parents were a big help on the project. My teachers were also a huge help because they gave me encouragement and support. Both my parents and my teachers were very proud of me when I was chosen as the Invent America! winner for the state of Wisconsin. I think I was in too much shock at that time to feel anything!

Now I realize that being selected a state winner was a big accomplishment for me. I was surprised and happy at the same time. Going to Dearborn, Michigan, to compete for the regional award was the best. It was unbelievable for me to find out that I was the only girl competing at my level. Even though I didn't win the competition, it was really fun to see the other kids' inventions. It gave me an idea of what others my age are interested in and what they can accomplish.

I guess you could say that the process I went through to succeed was very tough, and it took a lot of work. It's hard to explain just the

Jennifer Donabar and her Electro-Lock

way it makes you feel inside when you invent something. It's great the way everyone treats you and all the praise you get from people. It just makes you feel so proud of yourself. From the beginning, however, you have to have a positive attitude, faith, and hope. Most importantly, you have to believe in yourself.

I haven't really thought about getting a patent, or even putting my invention on the market. A patent would be a good idea, because then no one could use my idea. If they wanted to, guess who they'd have to pay? Me! Now that I think about it, maybe I really should patent my invention. Should I market my invention? One woman at Invent America! suggested that I market my lock. She said it would really help older people and people with disabilities who have a hard time with complicated locks. But there would have to be enough people to buy the product.

My advice to any and all young women is to always be yourself. Express yourself in everything you do and to everybody you are around. Also, if you want to improve the quality of something, or invent something, just think of something that would make your life and everybody else's life easier.

Jennifer Garcia

THE VACUUM DIRT MAT AND MORE

Fifteen-year-old JENNIFER GARCIA lives in Newark, New York. She is a tenth-grader at Newark High School.

Jennifer enjoys playing sports, including soccer and basketball, and is on the junior varsity soccer team. She plays the drums and is a member of both the school band and jazz band. She enjoys listening to alternative music and some classical music. Jennifer also collects ceramic pigs and has over ninety in her collection.

Jennifer lives with her parents, Gary and Kathy Garcia, and her nineteen-year-old-sister, Dawn. The family has four pets—two cats and two English bulldogs.

---

*W*HEN I WAS IN SEVENTH GRADE, I HEARD ABOUT the Invent America! contest and thought it would be interesting and fun to enter. Coming up with an idea for the contest was very hard. I tried to think of problems that needed to be solved. It seemed like everything I thought of was already invented.

A teacher at my school was very helpful. She encouraged me to keep thinking about what problems my family, friends, and I had in daily life and what I could do to solve them. Coming up with the problem to solve was definitely the hardest part of the invention process.

At the time, we had recently moved into a new house that did not have a paved driveway or lawn. My mom was always asking me to

*Jennifer
Garcia*

vacuum up the dirt I had tracked in from outside. I would wipe off my feet but would still get dirt on the floor. I decided I needed to also vacuum the bottom of my shoes. It seemed better to vacuum my shoes than the whole kitchen floor.

Combining a welcome mat with a vacuum cleaner seemed like a good solution. I wanted to invent a mat that activated a vacuum underneath when someone stepped on it. I went to the library and looked to see if anyone had already invented this kind of welcome mat. I found out no one had.

I first worked on a switch mechanism for the mat. My dad was a big help. He showed me what a switch looked like and how it worked. We bought a switch, but it took a long time to find the right sensitivity for stepping on the mat. When the switch sensitivity was too low, the mat would turn on when our cat walked on it. When the switch sensitivity was too high, the mat wouldn't turn on when I stepped on it.

I also found I had to have more holes in the floor mat for the vacuum to work well. The more we tried the invention, the more improvements I made. I learned that it takes a lot of testing and creativity to come up with a final product. My dad helped me cut the wooden housing for the dirt mat. I wanted the vacuum dirt mat to look good as well as work properly, so I sanded and stained the wood.

I named my invention the "Vacuum Dirt Mat." When I showed it to everyone, they said, "Why didn't I think of that?" Sometimes the best inventions are right in front of us, staring us in the face. We just have to keep looking for them. I'm glad I didn't stop trying.

I entered the Vacuum Dirt Mat in my school's invention competition and came in first place in my grade. My teacher sent my name and the worksheet detailing my invention and the invention process to the state group of judges for Invent America! A few weeks later, Invent America! notified my school that I was the winner for the state of New York. The company invited my whole family to Boston for the Northeastern competition.

Jennifer Garcia and her Vacuum Dirt Mat

Although I didn't win, I learned a lot more about inventing by talking to the other inventors at the competition. I also gained confidence by having to explain my invention to the judges.

I would like to patent my invention, but getting a patent takes a lot of money.

This year, I invented the "Uncopy Machine," a machine that erases photocopies. It is an invention that is a personal recycling machine. Using a special ink, you write on a piece of paper. To "uncopy" the writing, you just roll the paper through the Uncopy Machine mechanism. The machine's rollers apply a second chemical to the paper that dissolves the ink. Once the paper is dry, you can reuse it. I found the formula for the disappearing chemical in a chemistry book. The chemical is economical and would be useful for any home or office. I won first place at my school for this invention.

My advice to other inventors is just to try. Don't give up, even if things are really hard. Always remember that even if you are young, you can always think of things grown-ups can't.

THE POCKET DIAPER AND MORE

CHELSEA LANMON *is a nine-year-old fourth-grader who lives in Hamilton, Texas. She attends Ann Whitney Elementary School. School is fun for Chelsea; her favorite subjects are math, science, and reading—especially poetry.*

She has a three-year-old sister, Lauren, and two brothers—Bradley is eleven and Corbin is five. Ginger, her mother, stays home and takes care of Corbin and Lauren. Her father, Herman, owns an auto repair business.

Chelsea likes to do gymnastics and play house with her friends. She also likes to work with the computer, jump on her trampoline, and play with Lauren. At home, Chelsea has chores to do. She helps her mom with the little kids and the housework—but most fun of all is helping to bake cookies.

I NAMED MY INVENTION THE "POCKET DIAPER" AND made it in kindergarten when I was five years old. I got the idea for the Pocket Diaper when my little brother, Corbin, was a baby. Every time my mom changed him, I had to get the powder, wipes, and diaper. I wanted to find a way to get everything at once so I wouldn't have to be going back and forth for them.

The Pocket Diaper saves time because you have everything you need to change a baby in one place. Since there is less packaging for the

*Chelsea
Lanmon*

different products, it also saves money and helps the environment. With everything in one place, the diaper bag is easier to pack and stays neater.

When I started making my invention, I thought of several ways to create it. I tried putting the powder and wipes inside the diaper, but they would fall out. I thought of sprinkling some powder inside each diaper, but some parents might not like as much powder, or they might not use powder every time they change the baby. The powder would also be messy.

I decided to put the powder inside a "puff" made out of a dry baby wipe. I put the powder in the middle of a baby wipe, folded over the wipe, and sewed around the edges, kind of like a pillow. I poked small holes in the cloth with a fork so the powder would come out a little at a time. At first, I wrapped the baby wipe in a piece of foil. Later, I bought wipes that were already in individual packages. I made the "pocket" by cutting some of the outside covering from another diaper and attaching it to the new diaper with double-sided tape. The "pocket" peels off, and the wipe and powder puff are handy and ready to use.

My parents helped me with the cutting and some of the writing, since I was only five when I was making my invention. I did a survey of mothers with babies to find out if they would buy my Pocket Diaper and what they thought of the idea. Most people said they liked it, and they wondered why nobody else had thought of that. People always wonder why they didn't think of a good invention first. Most inventions are really simple and anyone could think of them, but it is the most fun when you think of them first.

My parents and I decided we wanted to get a patent on the Pocket Diaper so that we will be able to sell it. We got a patent pending on the diaper when I was six; when I was eight, the patent was issued. It is Patent Number 343,233. When my mom showed me the patent, I was really happy. I don't think many girls my age have patents, and that makes me proud.

We are working on marketing my Pocket Diaper. A marketing company has sent drawings and information about it to several companies, and we are waiting to find out if they would like to buy it. I would like to go with my mother to show the diaper to companies that could make and sell it. I could tell the companies how it works and why

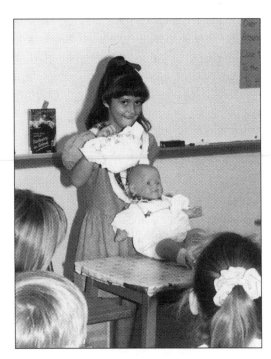

Chelsea Lanmon demonstrates her Pocket Diaper

it would be a good idea for them to sell the Pocket Diaper. The companies would be able to make some money because of my idea, and they would pay me some money, too. I think that someday moms and dads will be able to buy Pocket Diapers in the stores.

I entered my invention in the national Invent America! contest and won first place—and I was only in kindergarten. Because of that contest and my invention, my picture appeared in magazines and newspapers, and I got to go to places I'd never been, like Washington, D.C., and Chicago. When the people from the TV talk show, "Jenny Jones," called and asked me to be on their program, I was really excited. I was kind of nervous when the show started, but I relaxed and had a good time. A few weeks later, when someone called from "The Oprah Winfrey Show," we just couldn't believe it. I was really glad I was used to telling people about the Pocket Diaper so I wouldn't be nervous.

Showing my invention to reporters and important people helped me to know that I am a good speaker. It gave me confidence. If someone asks me if I'm shy, I say, "I couldn't be, I was on TV!" I think anyone who makes an invention she is proud of will have more confidence because of it.

I would like to tell other girls that inventing is fun. I think that girls are great inventors, even though most of the time people think of boys being the inventors. I got to see other girls with their inventions when we were in Washington, D.C., and their ideas were really good.

I have made an invention every year I have been in school. In first grade, I made an attachment for an iron called the "Sleeve Smoother." My invention makes it easier to iron sleeves, especially the kind of puffy sleeves on some of my and my sister's dresses. The attachment is shaped like a lightbulb and fits on the front of an iron. The "bulb" is made of aluminum, and it heats up when the iron gets hot. Then you set the iron up and slip the sleeve over the bulb. You can move the sleeve around, and it comes out puffy, not creased.

I entered the Sleeve Smoother in our school's invention contest and I didn't get any place at all. I was sad that I didn't win, but I was still glad I made an invention. I knew my idea was good, and it was fun to work on and think about my invention. I also had a good time showing it to people.

In second grade, I invented the "Super-De-Duper Ice Cream Scooper." The scoop has batteries in the handle. When you turn it on, a heating grid in the scoop part gets warm. After the scoop is heated, it glides through ice cream even if the ice cream is frozen solid. I won second place in our school invention contest for my ice cream scoop.

In third grade, I invented a heat and smoke sensor for frying pans that would help people know if a grease fire may be about to start. I entered this invention in the school competition but didn't place.

I don't know what will be next, I just know that I am going to keep on making inventions and other girls should, too. When one person makes a good invention, it makes others want to invent. I made my first invention because I knew that my big brother, Bradley, liked to make inventions for school. Someday my little brother, Corbin, and my little sister, Lauren, will make inventions, too. They will probably want to invent things because they have watched Bradley and me making our inventions every year. They know that we have fun when we invent. I will tell Lauren that girls are great inventors and I will help her with her work, especially when she is in kindergarten.

All girls should remember that they can be inventors. Also, you don't have to enter a contest to make an invention. You can think of inventions anytime. All you have to do is find a problem you want to solve, or ask other people what bothers them, then start thinking of ways to solve the problem. Inventions don't always have to be brand-new things. They can be ways to make old ideas better, like putting a pocket on a diaper or a heating grid in an ice cream scoop. After you make your first invention, you'll want to make many more. Just try it.

Karen Schlangen

THE UMBRELLA REDESIGNED

KAREN SCHLANGEN, 26, grew up in La Crescent, a small town in southeast Minnesota located on the Mississippi River. She is the only daughter of Andrew and Lynne Schlangen. Karen was born in March, 1969, and graduated as Valedictorian of the Class of 1987 at La Crescent High School. After a summer spent as the second Princess of La Crescent's Apple Festival, Karen traveled up the Mississippi River to the University of Minnesota in Minneapolis and St. Paul.

In her years of college, she was active in numerous student and community organizations, and won first and second place in two different national design competitions with two different inventions. Karen was named also to USA Today's All-USA College Academic Team—1st Team, and graduated with a Bachelor of Arts, cum laude, *in Psychology and a Bachelor of Mechanical Engineering,* magna cum laude. *Currently, she works for Kimberly Clark of Neenah, Wisconsin, as a mechanical engineer.*

$\mathcal{J}$T WAS CHRISTMAS NIGHT, 1991, AND I LAY IN BED unable to get to sleep. As I lay there, I remembered a conference I had attended a few years ago. Professor Ferdinand Freudenstein gave a talk entitled "An Analysis of the Scissors." At first, I had thought: "The scissors have been around forever and work just great. What am I going

Karen
Schlangen

to learn by listening to this talk?" Twenty minutes later, I sat in complete awe. Professor Freudenstein was able to look at scissors in a totally new and different way.

I started thinking about everyday objects that most people take for granted. Eventually, I thought, "Hey, the umbrella has been around forever. I'll bet a new design would make it work better." I wasn't sure how I would make it work better, but at least I had an object and a design challenge.

Next, I lay in bed wondering how I could improve the umbrella's spider web-like design. Once again my memory wandered, this time back to the summer of 1991. My friend and I were in a store, playing with a new product and trying to figure out how it worked. It was a shade for a car's dashboard. A nylon material covered a large metal ring. When I held the ring in a certain way and made a simple motion, it flipped into three smaller circles. With another movement, the three circles sprang back into one larger ring so quickly it startled us both. I was fascinated by the mechanics of this contraption. Somehow, I thought, I could use these metal rings to provide the shape for my new umbrella.

The next day, I examined an umbrella and found some design problems. First, the place of maximum protection from the wind and rain is underneath the center of the dome. But a central pole is in this space and the umbrella user must stand to one side.

The second problem is the umbrella's tendency to flip inside out. Many people have experienced a rainy, windy day when a gust of wind comes up from underneath their umbrella, forcing it to flip.

The third problem is that thin metal extensions hold the edges of the umbrella in place at eight stress points. Many times, the stitching between the extensions and the nylon fabric comes undone, and the umbrella becomes unusable.

Instead of using eight extensions, my invention uses a metal ring and two curved linkages to create a dome shape. With a single motion, you move the linkages at the same time and open the umbrella. When you no longer need the umbrella, you move the linkages again, and the umbrella folds up into three smaller circles about the size of Frisbees.

My new design solves the problems I found in the present umbrella. I was able to put the handle off to one side so the user can stand directly under the center of the dome. The linkages are strong and prevent the umbrella from flipping inside out. I eliminated the eight connections to the nylon fabric to provide better reliability. Also, the flat Frisbee shape of the closed umbrella is much easier to fit into a briefcase or backpack than the present design.

When I tell people that I've redesigned the umbrella, their first reaction is "Why? It's always been the way it is and it works just fine." Then I tell them of all the problems with the present design. When I describe my design, I most often hear, "Hurry up and make those, Karen. I want to buy the first one!" It's kind of fun to talk to people about my invention, because everyone has a bad umbrella story.

Through the University of Minnesota, I have received a patent on my invention. I'm in the process of licensing the patent to a company that will mass-produce and market this new umbrella.

An invention is something new, something no one has thought of before. The umbrella has been around for many years. No one has ever redesigned it. To me, that fact was like a neon light flashing "Opportunity!" I thought of my invention by bringing together past

information and experiences in a unique and creative manner—and
I didn't listen to the little voice saying, "It won't work. It's always been
done this other way."

Most people are used to thinking about the familiar. When they
hear about a new idea, they are skeptical and may doubt that a new
idea or invention will work. Don't let other people's doubts discourage
you or get you down. An important part of being a successful inventor
is self-confidence. If you let someone else's negative opinion dissuade
you, you'll never reach your full potential. Have faith in yourself
because you can do it.

People always say that it's the simple ideas that are truly the
ingenious ones, because millions of others have already overlooked
them. Take off the blinders and never think that an idea is crazy. If one
idea doesn't work, don't get discouraged. Get back up and start again.
If people call your idea crazy, it's probably because they don't understand it, or because they're jealous that they didn't think of it first.

*Karen
Schlangen
and her new
umbrella
design*

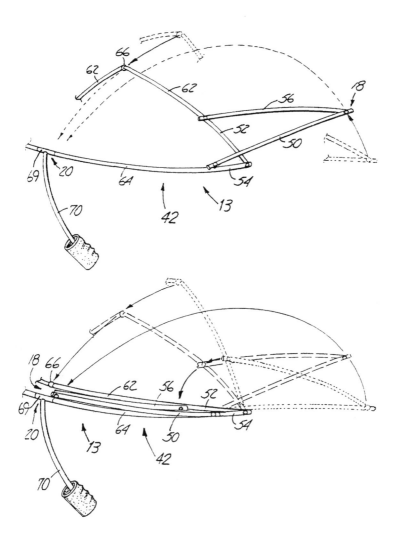

Patent drawings of Karen Schlangen's umbrella design

CONVENIENCE INVENTIONS

Questions to Think About, Ideas to Try

1. Inconvenience often sparks ideas for inventions. Brainstorm a list of items that are inconvenient for you, your family, your friends, older people, small children, or people with disabilities. What items in your list could you improve through changes or new inventions?

2. Think about a problem you, your family, and friends face in your daily lives. How could you make it easier? How could you get rid of it altogether? Figure out what you could do to solve the problem.

3. What items would be easier or more fun to use if they were smaller, larger, or a different color? What items would be easier or more fun to use if they could talk or make noise, or if they were made of different materials?

4. Look at an everyday object from a different point of view. How could you improve that object? How could you redesign the object to make it work better?

5. Read more about female inventors and their struggles to believe in themselves. You can find other books written by and about inventors at the local library. Look through the "Books to Read" section in Part Three of this book for a list of titles to get you started.

WORK-SAVING *Inventions*

Melissa Jo Buck

THE MOP HEAD COVER AND MORE

Fourteen-year-old MELISSA JO BUCK is a freshman at Mehlville Senior High School in St. Louis County, Missouri. Melissa was in the gifted program at Trautwein Elementary and took enrichment classes at Washington Junior High School. She is an honor roll student who was named an Outstanding Student two years in a row at Washington Junior High. She was also a member of the Spirits pom-pom team and the Drama Club. Currently, Melissa is taking advanced classes in science and mathematics and is looking forward to participating in cheerleading.

Melissa's father, Albert, is a banker; her mother, Barbara, is a part-time student. Melissa's brother, Al, is a freshman at Iowa State University.

Melissa is an avid reader. She also enjoys shopping, going to the movies, sailing, and vacationing in Florida.

$\mathcal{M}$Y INVENTING STARTED WHEN I WAS IN THE fourth grade. I passed the test to get into a program called STRETCH (Supplementary Teaching Resources for Educationally Talented Children), our district's gifted program. STRETCH students spend a few hours each week outside the regular classroom, doing activities to develop good thinking skills. We were doing a unit on problem-solving, where we had to find a problem and create a product to solve it. At the

*Melissa Jo
Buck*

end of this unit, we were going to display our ideas at our school's Invention Convention.

I thought of our kitchen floor, which has a pattern in it. Dirt gets into the pattern and becomes very hard to remove. My mom has to clean the floor by getting down on her hands and knees and scrubbing. I chose to create an invention that would help my mom clean that floor.

When she is mopping, Mom uses water, cleaner, and a mop. There is not much I can do with water, and I'm not a chemist—I couldn't change the cleaner—so I had to change the mop. The rubber head on our mop could not sink into the pattern of the floor, so that's where I started. Mom and I bought some different types of cloth and sponges to try on the floor. I tried several materials, including a sponge that I cut so it would have high and low spots in it. I hoped the high spots would get down into the floor's pattern, but that idea didn't work. Eventually, I found that terry cloth wrapped over the sponge mop worked the best. The loops in the terry cloth really got down into the pattern.

My next problems were to figure out how to get the terry cloth on the mop head, make it stay on during use, and get it off again to be washed. I had the idea that a tube of terry cloth would be easy to work with. Mom suggested that I use a tube sock turned inside out. I measured the mop head and cut the tube sock to the right length.

*Melissa Jo
Buck and her
Mop Head
Cover*

I finished the cut end with elastic so the end wouldn't stretch out of shape. That end hung open when it was put on the mop, however, and it looked terrible. I fixed that problem by putting Velcro on the end, so it could be closed after it was on the mop head. I also made openings in the sock so the handle and the connecting points of the sponge refill could attach to the mop.

Next, it was time to test my invention. We waited until the floor got monstrously dirty. I picked out two areas to test mop. In the first area, I mopped with a plain mop. I waited until that area was dry and looked to see how much dirt was left on the floor. In a different area, I mopped with the terry cloth-covered mop and waited until that area dried. It was obvious that the area on which I used the mop cover was much cleaner. Then I used the terry cloth-covered mop on the first test area. I wanted to see if I could clean the dirt that the plain mop had left behind. Once again, I was successful.

All that I had left to do was set up a presentation for the Invention Convention. I named my invention the "Mop Head Cover" and used before-and-after photos of each test. In my presentation, I described the steps very similar to the way I described them above.

You should know a little more about the Invention Convention to fully understand what is going on. All of the kids in the STRETCH program, grades four through six, are required to enter an invention. If they don't, they can't be in the STRETCH program. When I invented the Mop Head Cover, I was ten years old and in fourth grade, so I was extremely nervous about competing against kids one and two years older than me. The convention has several different categories. For example: household, school, personal, yard, and other.

Like any inventor, I was nervous about presenting my invention. I had proved that the Mop Head Cover really worked, but would the judges believe it? Apparently they did, because I won the Best Invention Award in the Household Division. Although I didn't win the top prize at the convention, Best Overall Invention, my family, friends, and I were still very proud.

I didn't abandon my invention after the convention, however. My parents and I went to an attorney to get my product patented so that no one else could make or sell this product. Although it sometimes takes a very long time to get a U.S. patent, I received mine in about a year. I have even had articles about me and my invention in two local papers. Now my family and I are looking for a company to license and manufacture the Mop Head Cover.

I have also spoken at a couple of Invention Convention Kick-Offs. The Kick-Offs are where all of the fourth-grade and any new fifth- or sixth-grade STRETCH students learn about the Invention Convention. I really must thank all of the STRETCH staff for letting me speak, and for everything that they helped me with. It was really fun.

The product I invented in fifth grade was a scrub brush with a long, flexible handle. My idea was to have the handle bend into different positions for reaching into hard-to-clean areas, yet be strong enough to really do some good scrubbing. I wasn't able to find the right material from which to make the handle, so that invention didn't work out well.

My idea in sixth grade was called "Desk Pockets." I used several different-sized pockets for holding things such as pencils, crayons, scissors, and rulers. I sewed the pockets to a base that could be stuck on the underside of my school desk lid, but removed easily. I used straps fastened with Velcro to hold things in the pockets. I thought this invention would help elementary students keep their desks neater. I was given an Honorable Mention at the Invention Convention for this idea.

I haven't had all of my inventions patented. One huge drawback of the whole process is that applying for a patent costs a lot of money—but someday that debt might get paid with the earnings from the Mop Head Cover. I haven't stopped inventing, either. Just recently, my mom and I started working on a new idea, which I can't talk about yet.

My advice for any future inventors is that if you have enough determination, you can accomplish practically everything. You never know when that good idea could come. Don't let it escape you…write it down. You don't have to invent something totally new. You could improve an object that already exists, like I have.

It doesn't matter how simple your invention is, just as long as it works. I have enjoyed sharing my experience with you. I hope that if you're inventing something, you'll do well in your process.

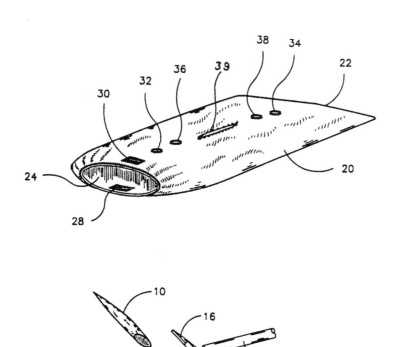

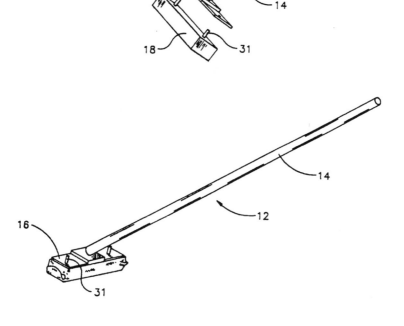

Patent drawings of Melissa Jo Buck's Mop Head Cover

Stefanie Lynn Garry

THE ADJUSTABLE BROOM

STEFANIE LYNN GARRY, 10, was born on October 17, 1984. She and her family live in New Orleans, Louisiana, where she is a fourth-grade student at Holy Name of Jesus School. Stefanie's mother, Jeanette, is an elementary school teacher. Her father, Bob, is a microbiologist at Tulane University in New Orleans. Stefanie has a twin sister, Katie, and a younger sister, Courtney.

Her favorite subjects in school are science and reading. Her main interest outside of school is gymnastics. She is a member of the River-bend Gymnastics Competitive Team and practices three to four times a week. She also enjoys swimming, bicycle riding, and singing in the choir.

When she was six years old, Stefanie and her family lived in Hamburg, Germany, for six months. She has traveled to many different countries in Europe including Italy, Spain, France, Denmark, England, Switzerland, and Poland. She hopes to be able to continue making new friends and traveling to new places in the future.

ONE SATURDAY I NEEDED SOMETHING TO DO. MY mother said, "Why don't you go outside and play or help Dad?" I played for a while, but became bored, so I looked around and decided to sweep the steps on our front porch. I found out, however, that my mother's broom was too big to use. I tried my little sister's toy broom, but it was too small. It was uncomfortable to bend over when using it.

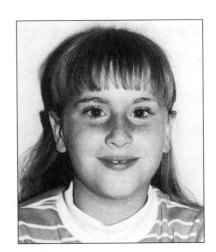

*Stefanie
Lynn Garry*

This seemed like a problem. My mother's broom was too big and my little sister's broom was too small. I decided that what I needed was an adjustable broom, one that people who were different ages and different heights could use. I also thought that an adjustable broom might be useful to sweep under hard-to-reach places, such as under a table, or clean high places, such as sweeping cobwebs off the ceiling.

A few days later at an assembly at our school, we were told that our school would be sponsoring another Invent America! contest. I had entered the contest the year before but had not won. This year, I was determined to come up with a good invention. The next weekend my father, my sisters, and I went to a workshop on Invent America! Many boys and girls were there. At the workshop, we learned about the inventing process and were told to look for problems or needs. We also talked about making diagrams and models of our inventions. We talked about the importance of keeping an inventor's log to document how we developed our invention.

I thought about my idea for an adjustable broom, and I knew it could work. I began to keep an inventor's log and wrote down my idea. I thought about how an adjustable broom might look and formed a picture of it in my mind. I needed to find out if anyone had ever invented or made anything like an adjustable broom before. I looked in the encyclopedia and different mail-order catalogs, but couldn't find

Stefanie Lynn Garry demonstrates her Adjustable Broom

anything like it. I also went to several hardware and department stores that sell brooms and household appliances and called a janitorial supply store. No one sold or carried an adjustable broom or had ever heard of one. Some people told me it was a good idea and they wished that someone would make one.

I had to work to develop my idea into an actual invention. I drew some pictures of my adjustable broom in my inventor's log. Mom helped me use a ruler to measure and draw straight lines. These drawings were very helpful, just like we learned in the Invent America! workshop. They helped me to figure out the right shape and length for the broom. My dad has a collapsible pointer he uses when he teaches. I thought this would be a good way to make the broom. I could make the broom handle in sections that could fit inside each other and be adjusted to different lengths. I wanted the broom to be able to shrink so it could be used by people who were shorter and fit into small places or under low places. I also wanted it to be able to expand so that people who were taller could use it without bending over, and people who were shorter could reach up to the ceiling to sweep away cobwebs or dust.

After I drew the diagrams of the adjustable broom, my family and I went to the hardware store to look for suitable materials to build the broom. I looked at various kinds of pipes and tubing and selected three different sizes that would fit inside each other. I picked plastic pipes because they would be the lightest material and the easiest to carry. I also bought a regular broom so that I could have the bristle part for my invention. I picked out some paint, and chose red, white, and blue for my colors.

When we got home, my father and I cut the pipe. We had to decide how long to make each piece. We worked together to figure out how to put the pieces of the broom together. After that, we painted each of the pieces a different color. It seemed like it would take forever for the paint to dry because I couldn't wait to see my finished product. The next day, we assembled the pieces and tested out my adjustable broom. It could shrink to about three feet in size and could expand to almost six feet, just like I had imagined.

I entered my adjustable broom into our school's Invent America! contest, and was happy to learn that I won for the second grade. Just think, someone else thought my invention was good, too! I sent my invention to the state competition. A few weeks later, I learned that I had won in the second-grade level for the state of Louisiana.

Many people have encouraged me to apply for a patent and market my broom. They said they wished that they had one to use. I have also realized that this broom would be useful for people with special needs. It could help someone in a wheelchair live more independently by making household chores easier. I have begun the process of applying for a patent and would love to see my broom sold in stores.

Making this invention taught me that there are at least three steps for success. First, you think that you can do it. Second, you set your mind to it. Third, you do it.

Anyone can be an inventor if you just put your mind to it. The hardest part of inventing is coming up with an idea that no one has thought of before. Be alert and look for a problem to solve. Then you have to think about a solution. Sometimes you won't come up with an idea or a way to solve the problem right away, but don't be discouraged. See if your solution will actually work. One way to do this is by making a model of your invention. If the model doesn't work at first, don't be discouraged. Remember, believe in yourself and keep trying. You can do it!

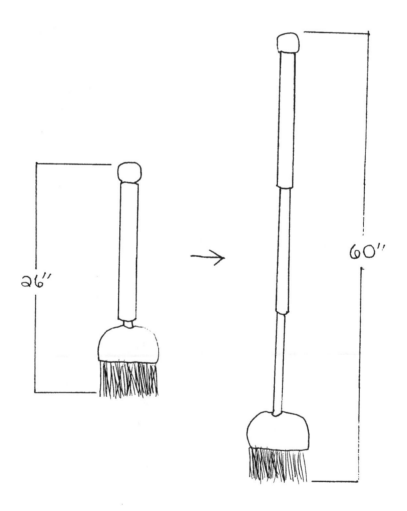

Stefanie Lynn Garry's drawings of her Adjustable Broom

KATINA'S CLOTHES SAVER

Twelve-year-old KATINA STEWART was born on March 20, 1982, in Savannah, Georgia, but she now lives in Upper Marlboro, Maryland. She is the only child of Jefferson and Stephanie Stewart. Katina is a seventh-grade honor roll student at the middle school in Prince George's County.

Katina has many interests, such as writing plays, acting, modeling, and reading. She has performed in several school plays, is a member of the Girl Scouts, and enjoys ballet and tap dancing.

She participated in the EXCEL 2000 Science and Math Summer Program, a pilot program sponsored by the National Aeronautics and Space Administration (NASA). The program is designed to make students aware of the career possibilities open to them if they choose to major in the sciences.

ONE OF MY MANY CHORES AT HOME INVOLVES doing the laundry on Saturday mornings. This is a dirty task, but someone has to do it—namely me. My bedroom is located on the second floor, in the far left corner of the house. In order for me to do my laundry, I must first find and sort all of my dirty clothes. Once I have identified all the items for the laundry, I must then carry them to the laundry room. The laundry room is located on the first floor, in the opposite corner of the house from my room. When I reach the

Katina Stewart

washing machine, the hard work is over. My goal each laundry day is the same: to make it to the laundry room in as few trips as possible. I didn't often reach this goal, since most of the time my laundry basket was filled to the top. I usually found myself collecting lost items trailing down the halls.

My fifth-grade teacher informed my class that everyone was required to invent something useful for the Invent America! contest. I began wondering what item I could invent. I thought about this until the following Saturday morning, when it was, yes, you guessed it right, laundry time. That morning, when I was carrying the second basket filled with clothes down the stairs, it hit me like a wildfire. I had an idea for the invention contest! I stopped at the bottom of the stairs, put the basket down, and went to my room to get paper and a pencil to start writing down the ideas for my invention. I loaded the washing machine and set out to find the materials I needed to make my invention.

The idea really developed because I wanted to make laundry day a fun day. I decided that what was needed for me to make my laundry day more enjoyable was something to keep all of the items securely placed in the laundry basket. It took a few days to get the idea on paper and find the necessary materials.

First, I needed to define the problem: Carrying baskets completely filled with clothes often resulted in reaching the washing machine with only part of the load. Second, I needed to think of a way to improve the laundry basket I had. I thought of various ways to close the top of the basket without adding more weight to it. Then the idea to cover the basket with fabric took form. Third, I needed to find the materials to make my idea a reality. Fourth, I took a survey of various family members, including my parents, aunts, uncles, grandparents, and cousins, to see how they dealt with their overloaded baskets. Additionally, I asked them if they thought a basket cover such as mine could make a positive difference. After this quick survey, I found out that my invention could be very useful to many people. Last, I needed to document the process based on the format the school provided.

Once I identified the problem, I was able to proceed with making the cover. The basket was the easiest item to find, but the other items were a little more difficult. My mother and I visited a fabric store in order to find stretchable material and elastic. Once we chose the fabric, we were ready to begin producing my invention. We purchased one-half yard of knit material and one-half yard of elastic from the store.

Katina Stewart demonstrates her Clothes Saver

When I returned with the fabric, the next step was to find out how much material was needed to cover the basket. I used a ruler to measure the width of the basket. Once I obtained this figure, I added two inches for a seam allowance. I folded the material in half and marked it using the above measurements. I laid half of the top of the basket on the material. I measured the area with a ruler to make sure that I really did have a two-inch seam allowance. I marked the fabric in the shape of a semicircle and cut along that line. When I opened the fabric, it was a complete circle.

I pressed down the seam allowance with an iron to make stitching easier and sewed an inch-and-a-half wide casing. Then I pulled elastic through the casing. The result was a secure cover for the laundry basket, which I named "Katina's Clothes Saver."

This idea is relatively simple but, I have been told, very ingenious. At the Invent America! contest at my school, I was very impressed with the other students' entries. So you must realize my surprise when the principle told me my entry had won first place among the fifth-grade entries.

This was a very special project for me since both of my parents were my partners. Both of them encouraged me to design and develop the best Clothes Saver I could. My mother helped me find the materials; my father and I spent many hours working on the drawings for the invention. After I won first place at my school, my father and I worked even harder at completing the entry requirements for the state competition. The state competition committee requested a more detailed report of my invention, including pictures. I was very pleased to receive a letter that summer from the Invent America! contest committee stating that I had placed first in the state of Maryland competition. Additionally, they informed me that I would also receive a $200 U.S. savings bond.

I have one piece of advice that I would like to pass on to other young inventors, and that is: If you can dream it, it's certainly possible. So, turn your laundry day or any day into a first-place, prize-winning invention.

Emma Tillman

THE SELF-DRAINING ABOVE-GROUND SWIMMING POOL WINTER COVER

EMMA TILLMAN, 15, is a freshman at Union City Community High School in Union City, Indiana. At school, she participates in Student Council and is a member of the volleyball and basketball teams. She also plans to try out for the tennis team. Emma plays the tenor and baritone saxophones in the school band.

When Emma is not in school, she can usually be found at her home just outside of Union City where she lives with her parents, Dave and Cheryl Tillman, and her younger sister, Eva.

IT WAS FEBRUARY, 1993, WHEN MY SEVENTH-GRADE science teacher told our class that we had to make an invention for our science project, and if we wanted to we could enter it in the Science Fair. At first I thought that I could never make my own invention. I really thought it would be impossible, but our teacher said to just think of a problem that needs to be solved and then solve it.

I automatically thought about a problem I had had the previous spring, when I drained the water off the winter cover of our above-ground swimming pool. Draining the water was very hard work. For a week, I worked every day after school to drain off the water that had collected from the rain and snow over the winter months. I had to bail bucket after bucket of stagnant water off of the cover. I dumped the buckets in an area away from the pool so that the yard surrounding the pool would not have that stagnant odor. Slimy leaves in the water made the buckets very heavy to carry. For a week, my hands smelled like that water.

I thought there had to be an easier way to empty the water. I decided to invent a special cover for our pool that would drain the water by itself.

I knew that I had to make a cover that would drain automatically. At that time, I really wasn't sure what to use to make the cover, but I knew I had to make a model. After a lot of thought, I began to gather all of my materials to make my model. I thought that a one-and-a-half gallon ice cream tub would work well to represent the swimming pool. The winter cover was harder. It took a long time for me to think of something that I could use. I finally decided to use a shower cap. The drainage system was probably the hardest part to create.

Finally, after considering many materials, I thought that a piece of plastic screen would work well to represent a filter. The filter would catch the falling leaves. The filter is on top of a funnel, which is built into the pool cover. A piece of rubber tubing is connected to the bottom of the funnel. The tubing runs through the swimming pool and connects to an adapter mounted in the side wall at the bottom edge of the swimming pool. Connected to the adapter on the outside of the swimming pool is a hose. All of the water coming from the top of the cover drains through the hose and out onto the yard.

Once I selected all of my materials, I began to construct my model. It was fairly easy to put everything together. Then it was time to test the model. When I tested the cover for the first time, it didn't work. It had a lot of leaks. I got discouraged when I had spent so much time working on it and then it didn't work. I put off repairing it for a while. When I did decide to repair my invention, I had a lot of trouble waterproofing all of the places where things were connected. First I used putty, but that didn't work well. I then tried hot glue and it worked

Emma
Tillman

very well. I named my invention the "Self-Draining Above-Ground Swimming Pool Winter Cover." Now I was finished with my project and ready to show it at school, as well as enter it in the Science Fair.

On the day of the Science Fair, I set up my display and looked around at all of the other inventions. There were many really neat and creative inventions. When they announced the winners, I was very surprised. I was selected as the first-place winner for the entire seventh grade. The next day, my science teacher told me that I could send a report about my invention to the Invent America! competition. I was now competing at the state level. I didn't think I had a chance to win for the entire state of Indiana, but I was still hoping.

It was the middle of May when my teacher got a phone call from Invent America!, and they told him that I had won the state level competition. At that time, I was in gym class. My teacher came down to the gym and told the gym teacher that he wanted to see me. I had no idea what he was going to say. At first I even thought I was in trouble. When he told me that I was the Invent America! winner for the entire state of Indiana, I was really surprised. That whole day I was really amazed. I couldn't wait to tell my family about it.

A week later, I got some information through the mail that said there was a regional Invent America! exhibition that would be held at the

*Emma
Tillman with
the display
showing her
invention*

Henry Ford Museum at Greenfield Village in Dearborn, Michigan. The
officials wanted me to come and display my invention there for two days.
I went with my family. My teacher and his family also went. I got to see
a lot of very unique inventions made by kids in kindergarten through
eighth grade. It was a new experience displaying my invention for all of
the public to see. I was a little disappointed that I didn't win this contest,
but I still had a great time. Although winning is nice, I actually enjoyed
the process of inventing more than winning the contests.

One goal I still want to reach is to get a patent and get my model
made into a real self-draining, above-the-ground swimming pool winter
cover that would be manufactured and sold all over the United States.
Then people with the same problem I had could benefit from the use of
my invention.

E. Z. TOOLS
AND MORE

JAMIE LYNN VILLELLA, 11, is a fifth-grader at Centennial
Elementary School in Fargo, North Dakota. Fargo is a community of
74,000 people located on the border of Minnesota and North Dakota.
Jamie lives with her parents, Larry and Debbi, a brother, Larry, and two
sisters, Barbara and Stephanie.

Jamie enjoys reading, inventing, in-line skating, and doing
homework. She also collects dolls, trolls, and clowns. She volunteers at a
nursing home, where she received an award for volunteering more than a
hundred hours. She also helps her brother with his sprinkler business and
his efforts to encourage tree planting in North Dakota.

In September, 1993, Jamie was selected to be a member of the
"Super Mario All-Stars Team," which developed the Nintendo Kids'
Platform. The organization addresses issues of concern to America's
youth and presents those concerns to elected officials in Washington, D.C.

$\mathscr{I}$ HAVE BEEN AN INVENTOR SINCE I WAS IN KINDER-
garten. I usually get my ideas for inventions by listening to what other
people complain about, or from something that bothers me. When
I hear about or experience a problem, I think of ways to fix it. I keep a
list of all of the ideas I come up with during the year. My school has an

*Jamie Lynn
Villella*

Invention Convention each year, and I usually have more than one idea for an invention.

Before the Invention Convention, I go through my list of ideas and solutions and ask people which one they like the best. When I can't decide which invention is the best idea, I enter two. I let the judges decide if they like one of the ideas or don't like either one.

Sometimes I come up with inventions that other people think are silly, but I try them anyway. It doesn't matter if my inventions win the contest or not. I learn what people like and how to improve on my ideas. I also think of ways that things I already have could be made better. My family actually sits around, pointing at different things in our house and thinking of things we would like to change. Everything we have was invented by somebody, so we also discuss how we think the person got the idea to invent it. There aren't any right or wrong answers, but we've had some crazy ones. I think talking with my family helps me see things a little differently. I'm always thinking about how to change things, because I'm always looking for my next invention.

Here are descriptions of my inventions (so far) and how I came up with them.

Grow-A-Size Shoe. Invented at age five. This is a shoe that has an insert in it that is a size smaller than the outer shoe. When you outgrow the size of the insert, you pull it out, and still have the same shoe. This way, you get twice the wear out of the same pair of shoes.

I came up with the idea because my sister had outgrown a pair of shoes, but they still looked brand new. They were too big for me, but I put my own shoes on, and then put hers on over them. They fit, but they were not very comfortable. Still, it gave me the idea for a two-size shoe.

Many people thought this idea was silly, but I entered it in my school's invention contest anyway. It won first prize in the school contest and placed first at the tri-city contest. I received two blue ribbons and $10 for my first invention.

Clip Tack and *Hide-Away Hat.* Invented at age six. This was the year I had two inventions. The "Clip Tack" is a tack I attached to a clip. The clip would hold papers on a bulletin board without poking holes in the papers. The Clip Tack will also hold a bunch of papers, so you don't have to try to push a tack through all of them. I came up with this invention because I didn't want to poke holes in pictures that I wanted to hang on my bulletin board.

The "Hide-Away Hat" is a hat with a shaded visor that flips down from the brim of the hat, to keep the sun out of your eyes. I came up with this invention when I was outside and didn't have any sunglasses. The Hide-Away Hat won second prize at my school's contest.

Child Safe Cabinet Alarm. Invented at age seven. This invention has a switch that attaches to a cabinet and an alarm that is hidden inside a picture frame in another room. When someone opens the cabinet, the alarm goes off.

I came up with this idea when my little sister broke the "childproof" latch on one of our cupboards and opened the door. She was playing with things in the cupboard, and I thought there should be an alarm that would tell if someone was in a cupboard that they shouldn't be in. This invention won first prize and grand prize at my school, as well as first prize at the tri-city contest.

E. Z. Tools (E. Z. Vac and *E. Z. Shovel).* Invented at age eight. This is the invention that won the state contest. The "E. Z. Vac" and "E. Z. Shovel" have handles that are like a lawn mower handle, so you can use both hands, instead of one, when vacuuming or shoveling.

My mom and aunt have arthritis and were complaining about how much their hands hurt when they vacuumed. I noticed that a lawn mower handle lets you use both hands, and I thought it might be easier to vacuum if you could put a lawn mower-type handle on the vacuum. I designed a handle that would let you do that, and my mom said it really helped. I wrote to some doctors and to the Arthritis Foundation in Fargo about the idea. They all wrote back to tell me they thought I had a great idea. I thought of other things on which the handle could be placed. When my dad complained about how hard shoveling was, I decided a shovel could use the E. Z. Handle, too.

Jamie Lynn Villella with her E.Z. Tools

I am trying to get a manufacturer interested in my E. Z. Vac idea. Although I haven't applied for a patent on my idea, I'm still looking for ways to have my invention made because I think people could use it.

My principal asked me to tell other kids about how to come up with invention ideas and how to display entries at the Invention Convention. He called me an expert and told me that there were a lot of schools in the state of North Dakota that participated in the Invention Convention, so being the third-grade winner for the state of North Dakota is quite an accomplishment. I'm very excited about my prize, a $200 dollar U.S. savings bond, but I'm also going to enjoy the next contest.

Electronic Neighborhood Watch. I am busy working on my newest invention. I have come up with an idea that will help people escape from fires, floods, or burglars in their homes. The invention is called "The Electronic Neighborhood Watch." It is a weathervane attached to a wireless alarm system. The weathervane goes on the roof of a house. If there is a fire, flood, or burglar, the alarms inside the house will set off the rooftop alarm. A strobe light and siren will turn on, so the neighbors or a passing motorist can call for help.

I have already written to eight local fire marshals and police chiefs to get their opinion of my invention. So far, I have received three responses. The Fargo fire marshal said my invention has the "potential to reduce loss of life," because "if the person were unable to escape from the home or unable to call authorities, a neighbor or passerby could call for help quickly."

I came up with this idea after hearing of local fires that were discovered by people passing by them. The people passing by were able to alert the people inside the house that they had a fire. This invention will also work great if you're not at home and a fire starts. You wouldn't be home to hear your smoke detector go off, but your neighbors would know there was a fire and could call the fire department.

The Electronic Neighborhood Watch was awarded a first place trophy for fourth grade. It was also named the Grand Prize Winner for the highest point total in grades four through six. My invention was also awarded a first place ribbon at the Tri-City Inventor's Fair.

....

My parents have helped me a lot with my inventions because they always help me figure out how to make my ideas work. But the most important thing my parents help with is encouragement. They never laugh at my ideas.

Sometimes kids have a way of looking at things in a different way, and we come up with ideas that others may not have thought of yet. I think we're willing to do a lot of things, because we do them for fun, and we're not afraid to fail. I was told that everyone who invents something is a winner because they tried. I think that's what kids should remember. If you don't try, you won't know if you could have been the inventor of the next hula hoop. No idea is a bad idea, because it is an idea. Every idea leads to the next idea.

You learn a lot of things when you invent something. Art, science, music, marketing, economics, and a lot of other things are part of inventing. But the best part of it is, you learn these things without knowing you're learning them—because it's *fun*!

WORK-SAVING INVENTIONS
Questions to Think About, Ideas to Try

1. Think of the messiest, most unpleasant chore you have ever had to do. What could you invent to make that chore less messy and unpleasant?

2. Brainstorm some solutions to a problem you have with chores. Use Katina Stewart's steps to work your way through to your invention.

3. Are you left-handed? Do you know anyone who is left-handed? Look around at the things in your home or school that are made for right-handers only. Adapt an item designed for right-handed people so that left-handed people can use it as well.

4. Keep a pen and an Inventor's Notebook next to your bed. (You'll find out more about the Inventor's Notebook in Part Two of this book.) Write down your invention ideas—no matter how outrageous they may seem. Later, you can read through your list and pick an idea to develop.

5. Getting other people's opinions about their needs for a new product can really help you develop your invention. By asking questions, you can begin to learn about the flaws and strengths of your idea. Make a list of people you know who would be good consultants for your invention.

6. Emma Tillman said that she enjoyed inventing for its own sake more than winning contests. Write down the reasons you would like to invent something, and see if you can use them to reach your goals more quickly.

7. Get some friends together and look at things around your school and home. Try to imagine how the things around you were invented and why.

CONSERVATION Inventions

Meghan Renee Hatfield

THE DRIVER'S LICENSE NUMBER SCANNER

Ten-year-old MEGHAN RENEE HATFIELD loves to go to Holz Elementary School, where her favorite subject is math. She lives in Charleston, West Virginia, with her mom and dad, Monica and Mark, and two younger sisters, Makenzie and Mary.

Meghan plays piano and sings in the University of Charleston Children's Choir as well as her church choir. Her school activities include dances and participation in Invent America! contests. In the summer, Meghan and her family live at their lake house in Beckley, West Virginia. When she is there, she swims, jet skis, rides in the family boat, and enjoys her gym set. She especially likes to watch movies and go fishing.

ABOUT A YEAR AGO, MY MOM, MY SISTERS, AND I were at K-Mart in Charleston, West Virginia. The clerk was taking a long time because she had to write my mom's license number on her check. I asked why the clerk couldn't just stick the check in the slot and scan the license number in the cash register. My mom heard my idea and suggested that I submit it to the Invent America! contest at my school. I gave her a big smile and said I would.

I created a model of my idea by drawing a blown-up version of a driver's license on a piece of cardboard. I then looked in my reference

Meghan
Renee
Hatfield

book, *The Way Things Work* by David Macaulay (Houghton Mifflin, 1988), to see how a scanner number works and how to draw a realistic looking number.

My mom and I called friends all over the country to see if any other state was using a scanner number on drivers' licenses. We found that these numbers were not being used in the states we called. I also thought that a scanner number would help police officers to quickly identify people they pulled over for violations. If the police officers had computers in their vehicles, they could scan the license for information. The scanner sticker could include as little information as a person's driver's license number, or as much information as a social security number and address.

As I developed my invention, I used one of my dad's old licenses and put a scanner number from a grape juice jar on it to show my invention more realistically. I called my invention the "Driver's License Number Scanner."

I turned in my invention and waited nervously until January 11 (the day of judging). I had entered the Invent America! contest three times before and had never won, so I was very excited this year. The judges called me in, and I had to talk about my invention. They asked how I came up with the idea. I was very honest when I told them that sometimes, when my sisters and I go shopping with my mother, our impatience drives her nuts. I knew there had to be a faster way for my mom to get out of the checkout line.

At the end of the day, the sponsor of Invent America! allowed all the participants to go to the room where the competition was held. The judges awarded first through fifth place and participation awards. I went into the room, looked around, and saw a first on my display. I thought, "That can't be mine." I was so excited. My teacher was as excited as I was. I went home and told my mom—she was excited, too.

Later that month, I went to a convention in my county, where I shared my invention with other student inventors. Summer came. My school sponsor entered my invention into the state competition of Invent America! To tell you the truth, I almost forgot about it. At the end of August, when I returned home from my family's lake house, I heard my mom screaming. I ran down from my bedroom to see what the problem was. My mom was saying: "Meghan, you won, you won!" I was confused. I wasn't really sure what my mom was talking about.

As it turned out, I was the Invent America! third-grade winner for the state of West Virginia. I was so amazed. I was speechless. In the letter from Invent America!, I was told that I would receive a $200 U.S.

A driver's license showing one of Meghan Renee Hatfield's scanner stickers

savings bond. The school would have an assembly for me. Ever since then, I've been really excited about winning. Winning the savings bond will be neat, but even more importantly, I have the satisfaction of knowing I took an idea and followed through with it.

To all young women (girls too), here are some tips if you want to become an inventor.

1. Never give up when you're working on a project. If it fails, keep on trying.

2. If you lose a contest, don't be sorry if you know you've tried your best.

3. Keep your eyes and ears open for new ideas, but don't steal ideas from other people.

4. When presenting your inventions to judges, be enthusiastic.

5. Don't put off work until the last minute. If you do, your work will not be the quality it could be.

6. Don't share your idea until you've patented it, or until you've won a contest with the idea.

7. Never give up.

8. Think simple. Sometimes the most "obvious" inventions haven't been invented.

9. Most of all, believe in yourself.

STALK BOARD

JANA KRASCHNEWSKI is eleven years old and attends Burlington Junior High School in Burlington, Wisconsin. She is in sixth grade and enjoys all subjects. Jana plays trumpet in her sixth-grade school band and is on the student council.

Jana enjoys playing on the softball, volleyball, and basketball teams. She likes playing with her two pygmy goats, Cleo and Billy The Kid, and is active in 4-H. Jana is involved in several 4-H projects including goats, rabbits, poultry, veterinary sciences, vegetables, music, photography, and basketry.

Jana's mom, Judy, is a teacher, and her dad, Jeff, is a chemist. Jana has a nine-year-old brother named Jacob, a twelve-year-old sister named Julie, and a fifteen-year-old sister named Jennifer.

$\mathcal{M}$Y DAD COMES HOME WITH ODD PHRASES ONCE in awhile. One day he told us about the *vortex tube*, the *thermite reaction*, and *cellulose*. Cellulosic material is in wood, he said. He also said that cellulose is found in bamboo and cornstalks. I didn't pay much attention to him, but I still remembered what he had said.

Sometimes on Saturdays I clean my dad's office and chemistry lab. I do things such as filing and washing beakers. On the way home one Saturday, I spotted some large circular bales sitting in a field. When I asked what the bales were, my father said that they were cornstalks. Then we went to my grandparents' house for lunch, and I said that I wanted to make plywood out of those bales. If both wood and

Jana
Kraschnewski

cornstalks contained cellulose, couldn't cornstalks be made into plywood? I didn't see why not. It was then that I started my tests.

Those bales we saw were later moved off the field to a stack, which is a large area where the farmer puts the bales in rows on top of each other. We saw that, year after year, farmers collected the bales and stacked them but did not use them. "Stalk Board," my invention, would solve this problem.

To create my invention, I knew I needed some type of adhesive to hold the cornstalks together. I wrote to many companies asking about adhesives. Most just thought I was too young to work with adhesives because some are dangerous. The adhesive I was looking for in particular was phenol formaldehyde resin. It is a thermal setting adhesive, so it needs to be heated to work. It comes in a powdered form and is dangerous. It can cause skin cancer if it comes in contact with skin or lung cancer if it's inhaled.

Some of the companies I contacted also manufacture plywood. I wrote to them to find out what other adhesives are used in the manufacturing of plywood and oriented straw board. (*Straw board* is made of chipped wood compressed and glued together.) The companies weren't very informative. Only a few replied, and they didn't offer the information I was looking for.

Finally, I decided to do some tests with Elmer's Wood Glue. The tests worked! As it turned out, it didn't really matter that I didn't get much help, because I had solved the problem by using the most low-technology glue.

There are many steps to making Stalk Board. First, I collected cornstalks from a combined (*käm*-bined), but not plowed, field. (When farmers combine their fields, they use large machines to strip the leaves from the stalks and cut the stalks into sections at the knuckles or joints. Next, the sections are halved or fourthed, depending upon the stalk size.) My neighbor is a farmer, and I asked if I could collect some cornstalks from his field when he was finished combining. He said yes. Using a paint can opener, I took the combined stalks and separated the pith from the "shell," or sheeted material. (The *pith* is the soft interior that allows water to travel up and down the stalk.) I laid the four "shells" side-by-side and added my adhesive.

I added four more "shells" on top of the first four, but in the opposite direction. I kept adding layers of shells (called *plys*) and glue to achieve the board's desired thickness. Then I placed two steel plates on either side (top and bottom) of the layers of plys. I clamped the board together tightly using two eight-inch "C" clamps. I kept the clamps on the board for twenty-four hours.

After twenty-four hours, the compressed "board-like" material had jagged edges sticking out every which way. I easily solved this problem by using a saber saw to cut the edges evenly. That made the Stalk Board a finished product.

Before coming up with the perfect Stalk Board, I made eight boards. I didn't succeed at first, but I didn't give up. My third one was the first decent one I made.

Originally, I worked on this invention for my school science fair. Then I became interested in Invent America! and sent my log book to that contest. (The year before, my sister Jennifer had become an Invent America! national winner with her "Leaf Log.") My log book included all of my experimentation, letters to companies, research, ideas, testing, and much more. It was all typed and in a binder. It is a good idea to

Jana Kraschnewski's drawing of her Stalk Board

keep your work clean, accurate, and orderly. My English teacher helped me with revising and correcting the spelling in my log book.

A few months later, I found out that I was the fifth-grade winner for the state of Wisconsin. I went to Dearborn, Michigan, as a regional contestant. Unfortunately, it didn't go any further than that.

Stalk Board has moved on since then because I discovered a new way to make it. Instead of using combined cornstalks, I began using shredded stalks. Here's how I made the new Stalk Board.

First, I shredded the stalks using a shredder from my grandparents' neighbor. I placed the shredded stalks into a wooden form, which I set on a cookie sheet. (I used a cookie sheet so that when I put the shredded stalks in the oven, the pieces of shredded stalk wouldn't drop all over the place.) My dad, who is a chemist, was able to get me a small amount of phenol formaldehyde resin so I could try this adhesive on my new Stalk Board. I sprinkled some of it between each layer.

When all the layers were in position, I placed the top of the wooden form on the board. Using the two "C" clamps, I clamped the form and board together tightly. Next, I placed the form, board, and cookie sheet in the oven. (I put the forms in the oven because phenol formaldehyde resin needs to be heated to be an effective adhesive.) I experimented using different temperatures and different times. The average time length was fifteen minutes. The average temperature was 350° Fahrenheit. After twenty-four hours under pressure, I removed the clamps. The result was a well-compressed, sturdy, waferboard-like Stalk Board.

My research on Stalk Board would have continued except for a few problems. First, of the many companies that I wrote to requesting resin, the ones that did reply said I was too young to be handling such a harmful chemical. Second, all plywood and flakeboard manufacturers are too far away for me to tour and visit.

I am working on another invention called "Aluminum on Fire." I invented a chemical reaction by mixing Al (aluminum), NaOH (sodium hydroxide), and H_2O_2 (hydrogen peroxide). The mixture creates a tremendous amount of heat and some of the water boils off. The NaOH removes the oxidized coating that occurs naturally off the Al. Then the H_2O_2 oxides the aluminum, causing the heat. The byproduct is an aluminum hydroxide and aluminum oxide, neither of which are harmful to the environment. Nobody has done this reaction before.

I am continuing work on this project, possibly making it into a furnace to heat homes. I have found that I cannot run the reaction with aluminum cans, only with granules. I am working to make or find a solution to take the protective sealant off the cans. Removing the sealant will allow people to recycle cans at home.

I am also designing a logo for this invention. The logo is a picture of an aluminum granule that is on fire and screaming.

I performed this reaction at my school's Invention Convention. If this invention doesn't lend itself to be at least a two-year-long study, or if I find I don't want to work with it anymore, I will go on to invent something else.

My advice to any inventors is to not give up. I didn't give up when the companies I wrote to didn't respond. I didn't give up when experiments didn't work out at first. Sometimes the most obvious things work the best. Elmer's Wood Glue worked fine for my adhesive. I realized that it isn't necessary to have the most high-tech things all the time.

Here's how I learned to invent.

1. First, find a problem that you think needs to be fixed. This can take one minute or one day. Don't worry if you don't find a problem right away.

2. Write down your problem. State why it needs to be solved. Make people aware that this problem exists.

3. Brainstorm possible solutions. It doesn't matter if you don't think you can do them. Keep track of your ideas.

4. Organize your thoughts. Select the best two or three ideas. Think briefly about which would be the most effective and the most practical. Think about which one you're most capable of doing.

5. Keep a log book of all your data or information.

6. Do experiments on your idea. Write them all in your log book. Choose the experiment that turned out the best. Do the experiment over again. See if you get the same results.

7. Run several tests on the product. Make any improvements needed.

8. If your product is a model of what the real thing should be, make the real thing.

9. Once you feel that your final product is as good as it can be, make sure it solved the problem. Then work on applying for a patent, because you don't want anyone to steal your idea.

10. Once patented, your idea is ready to go on the market. You may choose to sell your patent. You may need professional help in this area.

When you have an idea, go for it! Work with it, and be persistent. By inventing something, you help to make the world a better place.

CONSERVATION INVENTIONS

Questions to Think About, Ideas to Try

1. Ask your teachers and principal about the kinds of things they see wasted every day at school. Survey your friends and their families or people in your community to determine what they see wasted at home and at work. Invent a way to make use of some of those things.

2. Do you recycle things at home, in your school, or in your community? Look at the processes used in those programs. Think about how you could improve the recycling process.

3. Brainstorm a list of activities or tasks that are time-consuming or test your patience. What could you invent to make these tasks go quicker?

4. Does your school have some type of invention contest? Look through the addresses of organizations and associations in Part Three of this book. Talk to your teacher or principal about organizing a contest and getting other students interested in inventing.

5. What obstacles have you encountered—or do you expect to encounter—as you invent? What plan of action will you use to overcome these obstacles?

FUN Inventions

THE TOOTH FAIRY LIGHT, THE SHHHH MACHINE, AND MORE

Ten-year-old KELLYAN COORS has lived in Aurora, Colorado, all of her life. She is the youngest of four children and has two brothers and a sister. She also is caretaker for a rabbit named Mr. Bugs, a Samoyed dog named Quita, a black Labrador retriever named Cinder, a hand-fed parakeet named Mrs. Michigan, and, at last count, twenty-four hamsters.

Kellyan is a fifth-grader at The Challenge School, a new school for academically advanced, motivated students. She especially enjoys her biology class, her mathematical problem-solving explorations, and her River Watch chemistry experiments. Kellyan thrives on learning how the world around her works. The dissection classes she took at the University of Denver increased her interest in the field of medical science.

She is active in gymnastics, swim team, piano, tap dancing, and Girl Scouts. She is also involved in Odyssey of the Mind, a program that encourages students to develop problem-solving skills.

Her parents, Kenneth and Virginia, and brothers, Kenneth and Henry, have encouraged Kellyan. But her inspiring mentor has been her sister, Elizabeth Brandon, who is also academically gifted and shares Kellyan's strengths in math and science. Her sister graduated from

Cornell University, and this is where Kellyan hopes to pursue her studies in medicine and one day become a family physician.

---

*M*Y LOVE FOR NUMBERS AND MY INTEREST IN science began when I attended preschool at Denver Montessori. The three years I spent there definitely affected my love of learning. I am a curious person. I enjoy investigating, exploring, and reading all about interesting things (like medical science and famous women), as well as doing math problems and science experiments. The people at the school helped me because they allowed and encouraged me to advance academically at my own rate, while they challenged me to explore and try all sorts of new projects. We took field trips to lakes and zoos. In the classroom there were books, games, and hands-on projects that covered everything from A to Z.

I've been an inventor now for several years. In first grade, I invented a blinking "Tooth Fairy Light" because I was concerned that the tooth fairy sometimes forgets to come by when someone loses a tooth. But with the Tooth Fairy Light, the child puts the light in the window of his or her room and the blinking alerts the tooth fairy as she flies around.

I began creating this invention by researching electrical circuits. First, I went to hardware stores, and then a pleasant man at a lighting store helped me make a simple circuit that I secured to a block of wood. My next task was to create a unique fairy to place over the light. I used a Styrofoam cone for my base, but upon testing whether the Styrofoam could withstand the heat from the lightbulb, it caught on fire! Well, back to the drawing board, as they say. Eventually, a glass cone tested out as being safe, so it became my base.

My grandmother took me to fabric stores, and I found the perfect gown material for my fairy's elegant outfit. I sewed it on my grandmother's sewing machine and even included a heart-shaped pocket on the gown for the tooth and the tooth fairy's wand. Next I developed the really important part: I wanted my tooth fairy light to

Kellyan Coors

blink, so I had to somehow interrupt the circuit. Once again, it was back to the lighting store. The patient man demonstrated how a flasher plug works. Fascinating! Inside the plug there is a metal piece that expands and contracts to make contact with the electrical current; therefore, the current is interrupted, and we have a blinking light.

The Invention Fair at my school that year was not Invent America!, so first-graders did not get judged, but I was thrilled to enter nonetheless. I created a poster with pictures showing my invention steps and the reason my invention served an important purpose. I had quite a crowd of adults as well as children around my table that night. Many kids wanted to immediately use my Tooth Fairy Light because they had missed a visit from the tooth fairy when they had lost a tooth. I was so proud of my first invention. Since I invented this light, many kids have used it.

I couldn't wait to start investigating for my next invention in second grade. (That year, the competition was an official Invent America! contest.) Throughout the year, I became more and more annoyed with all the noise in my classroom. When it came time for the Invention Fair again, I began exploring the world of sound by reading many books on the subject.

The complex nature of hearing intrigued me. The ear's interpretation of the intensity of sound is called *loudness*, and the degrees of intensity can be measured in units called *decibels* (dB). I also learned that the average conversation is around 60 dB, while an airplane taking off is 120 dB. Anything above 70 dB could cause hearing problems. I needed to make others aware of how constant noise, even if it is not extremely loud, is harmful. Constant noise can cause fatigue, headaches, tension, nausea, hearing loss, and crankiness. It is also difficult to learn in a noisy environment. My problems were: How could I make my classmates aware of noise levels? Could I make my classroom less noisy?

My solution hit me when an engineering friend gave me a decibel meter. I already knew how it worked. I decided to invent a "SHHHH Machine" that would monitor the noise level in the classroom and let the class know when the noise level was too loud for people to concentrate.

As my invention continued to evolve in my mind, I decided to connect the decibel meter to a blinking red light. When the noise level in the classroom reached 70 dB, I wanted the red light to automatically light up and begin blinking. Unfortunately, I couldn't figure out the electrical components to cause the decibel meter to electronically trigger the light, so it wasn't as perfect as I wanted, but I created the best invention I could.

Because I couldn't get the decibel meter to trigger the light, a person had to do it—a person designated as the Classroom Noise Monitor. I covered a piece of plywood with vinyl and secured the decibel meter to it with a screw. I pulled string through hooks that led to the "noise control" panel. Under the panel were messages like "Our ears are hurting!," "Sound—OFF," and "Too Loud." When the monitor notices the decibel meter reaching 70 dB or above, he or she pulls the string, reveals one of the messages, and turns on the flashing red light.

Even though my invention wasn't exactly as I had imagined, I was still proud of my accomplishment. I made my classmates more aware of noise levels because we used the SHHHH Machine in the classroom for the rest of the year. I took the decibel meter everywhere I went. I was amazed at how noisy many activities are. For instance, my piano playing was 80 dB.

I was delighted when I won second place in the Invent America! contest at my school. I still feel that every teacher would want my SHHHH Machine in their classroom, so that everyone can be aware of noise levels. Actually, this invention would be ideal in all environments.

As I said earlier, my love for numbers and my interest in science began while I was at Denver Montessori. While other kids learned their ABCs, I was doing multiplication. While I was in elementary school, I was mostly with boys because many of my girlfriends didn't seem to want to do puzzles, logic problems, and math. For awhile, I was confused; I shared their enthusiasm for books and creative writing, but many didn't like math and science.

In the third-grade gifted and talented math class at Polton Elementary School, there were only three girls and, of course, many boys. This made me furious. I began to wonder, "Why aren't most girls curious about math and science?" I noticed that some teachers didn't expect girls to be strong in math. Also, I noticed that boisterous boys often yelled out answers instead of giving girls a chance to answer. At the time, some of my friends looked at a math test and didn't even attempt it.

All of this information gave me a great idea. I needed to find a way to make my girlfriends want to do and enjoy math and science. I began by reading articles about women in math and science careers, and about girls not being encouraged to explore these fields. I read about gender bias in the schools, and how teachers did not know the needs of gifted girls. I thought, "Why not invent a game?" I went to the toy stores to make sure that a game like the one I had in mind had not already been made. I found that the games for girls were mostly about dating, shopping, and being beautiful. There really needed to be a game that challenged girls in intellectual areas.

Unfortunately, girls usually do not want to show off their math and science talents. Even so, I found many biographies of famous

Kellyan Coors (center) with her game

women who have achieved their goals in math and science, and this encouraged me to continue to work on my game invention. By talking to some of my girlfriends, I realized that, basically, girls have a difficult time taking risks. It's hard for some of them to try their best on a math test, raise their hands to answer questions, research and design an invention, find creative uses for common objects, and feel comfortable with the fact that they are smart.

After researching, I decided I would make a game called "Boys, Scoot Over! Girls, Advance to the Top!" I finally came up with this name the night before the Invent America! contest. I thought the name was a little long, but it described my game exactly: I wanted girls to have the confidence to get to the top of their classes in math and science.

I made the game with five kinds of questions, each on its own set of colored cards: math computation (green), math problem-solving (blue), science (red), famous women (orange), and take a risk (pink). Colored beads match the colored question cards, and these match the colored sides of the die. The game begins with a player rolling the die. According to the color on the die, the player takes a question card from the appropriate question box. If she gets the answer right, she takes a colored bead that matches the color of her question card and puts it on her pipe cleaner in front of her. Once she has answered three questions from the same category (her pipe cleaner will have three beads of the same color), she gets to move her playing piece up one level on the big pyramid in the center of the board.

The object of the game is to get to the top of the pyramid first. I used many books to write the question-and-answer cards, but the risk questions were the most fun to make up. Here are some examples of questions found in my game:

▶ Math computation: Write an equivalent fraction for 3/8 and explain your answer. (Answer: Varies, 6/16 or 12/32, etc.)

▶ Math problem-solving: Five students from Mrs. Taylor's class went on a science field trip Saturday. They traveled 234 miles in 5 hours and used 13 gallons of gasoline. How many miles per gallon of gasoline did the group average? (Answer: 18.)

▶ Science: What are the three common states of matter? (Answer: Solid, liquid, and gas.)

▶ Famous women: She was born in Central City, Colorado, and was one of the nation's first female doctors to receive medals and honors in medicine. (Answer: Dr. Florence Sabin.)

▶ Take a risk: You are a good math student, but the teacher never notices you. You have thirty seconds to act out how you would solve this problem.

The night before the Invent America! contest, I was very excited. I'd finished making the game, so I started on my description poster. I decided to put some of the articles I'd read about famous women and gender bias on the poster, along with the object and rules of the game. My table at the competition was a popular one. One teacher of gifted and talented kids from another school in the Cherry Creek School District spent at least an hour with me asking questions and showing her delight in my game for girls.

There were two judges, a man and a woman. Both were enthusiastic and wanted to know more about how I had come up with the name for my game. They enjoyed reviewing my long inventor's log. It was then that I realized there was a chance I would take a place in the contest. By the end of the evening, I had about nine girls at my table wanting to play. Once most of the people were gone, I was able to play several games with the group. I ended up taking first place in Invent America! that day.

Later, after my game had been entered in the state competition in Washington, D.C., I found out that I had been selected the third-grade winner for the state of Colorado and had won a $200 U.S. savings bond. Then, something that was truly thrilling happened. In the fall, I was notified that I had won the Ten State Regional Third Grade Contest and a $500 U.S. savings bond.

There are several people who helped me with my game. My parents and brothers helped, but my older sister, Elizabeth (Sissy) Brandon, and my friend, Nicole Grace, helped the most. Sissy really liked my idea and inspired me because she remembered what it was like when she was in elementary school and her friends didn't share her love for math and science. It wasn't until she got to Cornell University and started studying engineering that she was surrounded by female mathematicians. Although she was in New York while I was creating my game, she still called and wrote all the time to let me know she backed me a hundred percent.

Nicole is a friend who is a year older than me. She loves math and science, too, so we really have a lot in common. We even dissected animals together in a class last summer at the University of Denver. She helped me research some of the game questions. One of the things I've discovered is that it is great to have gifted girlfriends who think like I do; then I don't feel so strange.

My parents and I are looking into different options for marketing the game and copyrighting the name. We may try selling the idea to a big game company like Parker Brothers or Mattel.

Most recently, I have been researching the intriguing world of hamster breeding. Over the years, I have noticed that children and parents looking for hamsters wanted lovable, friendly creatures that were also unique in some way. After reading books on hamster breeding and genetics, I decided to experiment in order to breed hamsters with exceptionally calm temperaments and unusual colored Angora coats. I was not after the common white-bellied agouti; I wanted to invent a new variation. I am also experimenting with designing an inexpensive hamstery with mating and breeding cages and nest boxes. Keeping accurate records is a must, so I am inventing an easy, all-in-one system for recording mating dates, genetic profiles, breeding information, and other necessary details. The complicated world of genetics is fascinating.

I want to tell other girls that inventing is really fun and challenging. We all have ideas that would make life more fun, easier, or less messy. All you need to do is go to the library and read about things that are related to your idea. Also, there are always adults around who are very helpful and willing to help you with the complicated parts of your invention. It is such a neat feeling of accomplishment when you build something that no one else has built before. Winning is fun, too. I keep an invention log by my bed, and every time I think of an invention, I write it down. Putting your ideas on paper is the first step. From there, all you need is the courage and desire to make it work. Once you move beyond your fear of taking a risk, you'll realize that inventing can be really rewarding. You'll also realize that there are a lot of things that you were afraid of doing before, but aren't afraid of now.

HAPPY HANDS

Ten-year-old ELIZABETH LOW is a fourth-grade student at Barbara Bush Elementary School in Houston, Texas, where she is in the honors program.

Elizabeth likes to ride horses (English, Western, and bareback styles), roller-skate, and ice skate. She also likes to play with her animals, which include a rabbit named Bonnie, a cat named Cindy, and a dog named Lady, who all get along with each other.

Elizabeth's father, Richard, is a pediatrician; her mother, Susan, manages the office for Elizabeth's father. Elizabeth has an older sister, Jeanie, who likes to invent things, too, and two other siblings, William and Christensen. Elizabeth is close to her family and likes to go on fun trips with them. She would like to be an inventor when she grows up.

I HAVE ALWAYS BEEN INTERESTED IN INVENTING things. Each year in Houston there is an invention fair at one of the local malls. I try to think up something new each year to exhibit. I came up with the idea for a paperweight when I was four years old.

Several afternoons a week after preschool, I would go to my dad's medical office to visit and play with him. I found that the rubber gloves he wears when he examines patients are very elastic, and that I could form them into lots of interesting shapes if I filled them with sand. My dad began to wonder where all his gloves were going. I was taking them home and filling them with sand.

I worked with the sand-filled gloves and created all types of interesting shapes. I began to fill the gloves and then paint animals and flowers on them. I found that the gloves could be used as paperweights, supply holders, and office decorations. I came up with the name "Happy Hands" because I can make all sorts of happy shapes and because playing with them makes anyone happy. They are great stress relievers.

Armed with a few boxes of Happy Hands, I went to the mall to participate in the Houston Invention Society Exhibit. I was too young to be placed in any category, so they put me with the kindergartners. Much to my surprise, I won the entire fair against high schoolers and elementary kids.

I gave samples of my paperweight to the judges at the exhibit and to the news reporters and television camera operators. The next day, I appeared on several local news shows.

I knew I had an idea that was fun to play with, a catchy name, and a fun product. But before I could market my invention, I had to do what is called Product Testing and Research.

The original Happy Hands glove tended to be fragile if left in hot places. It would break, spill out the sand, and make quite a mess. After trying over a hundred glove types, I found one that was pliable enough

Elizabeth Low

to be stretched in all sorts of shapes, but durable enough not to break or come apart if left in a hot place.

The next problem was the texture and quality of the sand. Natural oils in the sand could eat through or discolor the rubber of the glove. Any pebbles in the sand could also tear the glove. So the sand in the glove had to be dry and sent through a strainer to remove any small pebbles. Another problem was filling the glove with sand. I used a special funnel to fill the gloves with a measured amount of sand. I also found that it was hard to remove all the air (to insure flexibility) and knot the end of the glove. I found that by using the handle on our garage door as a hook, I could secure and tie the gloves ten times faster than by just using my hands.

I made several Happy Hands and placed them on desks, on windowsills in the sun, and in boxes in a dark closet. (Two years later, I checked on them. They were still in the same pose I had left them and still pliable. The sand had not discolored them.)

Next came the problem of how to decorate the paperweights. Washable markers sometimes came off on the fingers of people who held the paperweights, and sometimes the colors ate into the rubber. For the paperweights that would be used only for display in offices and homes, a non-washable latex paint proved to be ideal and quite bright and cheerful. A company could even print a decoration or their logo directly onto the rubber.

The next problem was to see if anyone would want to buy the paperweights. I displayed the paperweights at a do-it-yourself show. At first, I didn't sell any because I had priced them too high. Then, when I lowered the price and offered a "two-for-one" special, the Happy Hands began to sell. From the show, I learned that the paperweights were sellable and sold best at a moderate price that still gave a good profit—and that people bought more of them when I sold them in pairs.

I found out there were two kinds of patents for which I could apply: *design* and *utility*. I received help with the patent process from the Houston Inventors Association. At first, I decided to go for a design patent, but later decided to go for a full utility patent, which would include the uniqueness of the idea and not just the design. With the help of a Houston Inventors Association patent attorney, I did a patent search to see if anyone had a similar idea. Finding none, I prepared a patent application. The patent office corresponded twice with requests for more information, which I sent. Applying for a patent is hard work. On an average, it takes at least twenty-four months of correspondence and research. While this goes on, the phrase "patent pending" protects the idea. This phrase means you can start developing the patent without worrying about someone stealing it.

My patent application was approved, and my patent was issued on March 1, 1994.

Woman's Day and *Kids R Us* magazines have contacted me about doing articles about me and my invention. A radio station in Iowa and a television show on CNBC have interviewed me. I also appeared at the Inventing New Products Exposition (INPEX) in Pittsburgh, Pennsylvania. Inventors from all around the world were at the fair. I won a gold medal in the toy category.

My sister, Jeanie, is also an inventor. Together, we came up with ten points for invention success, which I use to test the marketability of my inventions.*

Almost everyone who sees the Happy Hands wants one. When the Patent Office invited Jeanie to exhibit her invention at the Smithsonian Institution in Washington, D.C., I got to go along. The Happy Hands were a big success. I gave decorated Happy Hands to the Assistant Secretary of Commerce, the head of the Patent Office, and even government officials from Brazil. My Happy Hands were placed on the entrance table at the exhibit and wound up at tables throughout the exhibit. Several TV stations and reporters interviewed me; my picture and an article appeared in *Inventors' Digest* magazine.

The producers of the TV show, "Why Didn't I Think of That?," invited my sister and me to California. I gave Happy Hands to the production company and even sold two Happy Hands to the most famous other "hand" in show business: Thing the Actor, whose hand

---

* Jeanie Low's story appears on pages 116–121. The ten points for invention success appear on pages 120–121.

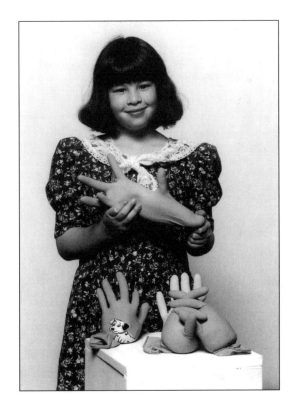

Elizabeth Low with some of her Happy Hands

plays "Thing" in the Addams Family movies. I autographed several of the hands.

Last summer, I attended the USA Inventors Exposition at the Smithsonian. A picture of Jeanie and me and our inventions appeared in the front page of the Style section of *The Washington Post*. The South African Invention Society is doing a two-page spread about Jeanie and me, and we're planning to go to Johannesburg to exhibit our inventions.

It is fun to show my Happy Hands to people and tell them about my invention. It is also fun to watch them play with the Happy Hands.

I am currently working on other inventions, including a flame-resistant mattress cover that can be used as a covering hood during a fire. My most recent invention is a lens that doctors can use in medical instruments. This lens could replace the need for doctors to wear their reading glasses.

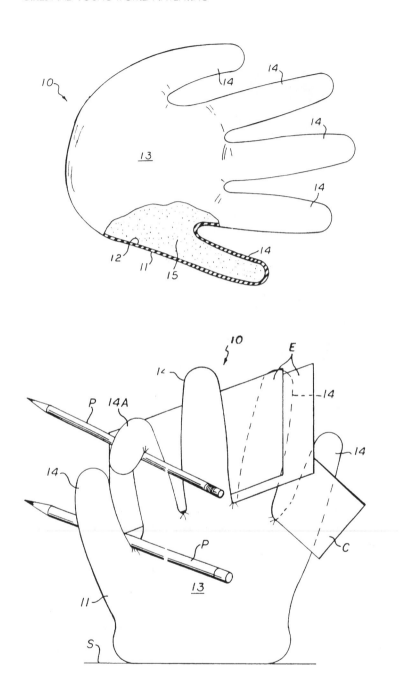

Patent drawings of Elizabeth Low's Happy Hands

ICE BLADES

EMILY MEREDITH TUCKER, 12, was born on June 4, 1982. She lives in Shaker Heights, Ohio, and is in seventh grade at Shaker Middle School. Her favorite subjects are math, reading, spelling, and art. Her interests are ice skating, playing the piano and saxophone, reading, and doing arts and crafts. She used to like horseback riding until she had an accident with a horse at camp. Emily also enjoys thinking of inventions and sometimes making them.

Emily is part of a stepfamily. She has a twin brother named Michael; two stepsisters, Ann and Kelly; and a stepmom, Karen, who is a real estate agent. Her father, Robert, is a lawyer. Emily also has three cats, Tipper, Choo-choo, and Carrot.

Emily hopes to be a veterinarian someday and maybe an inventor.

---

*I*T WAS AROUND THE END OF JANUARY, 1993, WHEN I began to think of an invention. I brainstormed for about a week and finally came up with an idea. I got my idea because I like to ice skate and in-line skate. I go to ice rinks a lot because my sister and brother play hockey and I figure skate. I also think that it is hard to tightly lace in-line skates. The invention that I thought of was ice skates that could be turned into in-line skates. My parents are always complaining that we grow out of our skates too fast, so this invention would solve the problem of having to buy both ice skates and in-line skates. Also, people would be able to go from ice skating to in-line skating quickly, without having to remove their ice skates.

Emily
Meredith
Tucker

I thought of how I could make my invention. My first idea was to clip wheels on to the ice skate. But I quickly learned the skate wouldn't be sturdy enough and the wheels would ruin the ice skate. While I was looking at the skate, I thought of clipping wheels on to the ice skate guard so you could just clip on the guard and in-line skate. But there was not a way to keep the guard on, and the skate wouldn't be sturdy enough, either. Then I thought of putting a wheel on a bolt, slipping the bolt through a hole in the guard, and putting another wheel on after the bolt was through the hole. (The bolt, I figured, would hold the wheel and the guard in place.) I had to decide how many sets of wheels I would need. I originally thought of having three sets of wheels on each guard because many in-line skates have three wheels.

In mid-February, I decided to make a prototype. I went to the hardware store and bought long bolts to go through the skate guard, wheels to put on the bolts, and nuts to hold the wheels on. Making the guard was not as easy as I had thought. I had to drill holes through the guard, put a wheel on the bolt, screw the bolts through the holes, and screw on nuts to keep the wheels on. I was concerned that the wheels would rub against the metal bolt and wear out, so I decided to use rubber stoppers next to the wheels. I decided I would only use two pairs

of wheels instead of three because that's all we could find at the
hardware store.

I was very excited about trying out my invention. I went with my
brother and sisters to an ice skating rink. When I got there, my sisters,
brother, and other people wanted to try out my invention. I told them
that they could try it after I did. After my first trial, I found out that the
nuts had come off the bolts. Later, after the others had tried my
invention, I found out something else: The bolts had bent from all the
weight of the skaters and the wheels didn't turn.

I went back to the hardware store and bought thicker bolts, then
went home and drilled bigger holes in the guard so the thicker bolts
would fit through the guard. I found out that the wheel holes were too
small and that the bolts would not go through them. So I had to drill
bigger holes in the wheels. I soon found out that the holes in the
rubber stoppers were too small, and I had to drill bigger holes in the
stoppers, too.

Next, I had to figure out how to keep the nuts on the bolts. My
dad explained to me how a bolt and nut work, and he showed me the
threads on the bolt and in the nut. A nut's and a bolt's threads fit
together perfectly, so if you ruin the threads on the bolt, then the nut
is unable to come off. I decided to ruin the threads on the bolts. I tried
it out again and it worked! The bolts didn't bend and the nuts didn't
fall off.

I learned an important lesson about inventing. I found out that
when you change some of an invention to fix a problem, you end up
changing most of it!

Shortly after making my invention, I thought of a name for it.
I was combining in-line skates (also known as Roller Blades) and ice
skates together, so "Ice Blades" was the perfect name.

I did research to make sure that my invention was new and
original. First, I visited many ice rinks throughout northern Ohio,
including Mentor, Euclid, CSC, Shaker, Garfield, Parma, and North
Olmstead. I went to these places to watch my brother and sister play

hockey. During the time I was there, I didn't see anything like my invention.

Second, I have ice skated for six years, and I have never seen anything like my invention. After I came up with the idea, I started to pay close attention to the kinds of guards that people used. I did not see anyone with wheels on their guards.

Just to make sure that there were no inventions like mine, I visited sporting goods stores over one weekend. None of the sporting goods stores sold anything like my invention. There were ice skates and in-line skates but no guards with wheels on them.

I also went to my dad's law office to use his computer to search patents. I searched five files and only one had anything like my

*Emily
Meredith
Tucker
demonstrates
her Ice Blades*

invention. In that database, which was called "Ice Skates With Wheels," I found thirty-six patents. I printed out a list of the patents and read through it. I found three patents that sounded like mine. I printed those three out and read them to see if they were like my invention. None of them were like it because they were not guards with wheels. Based on my patent search, I concluded that there were no other inventions like mine. I knew then that I had an original idea.

I was excited when I took my invention to school and shared it with the class. Everyone in school was bringing in an invention to exhibit at the Invent America! contest. I showed my class how I made my invention and how it works. Then I took it down to the gym and waited to hear the judges' decision on Friday, February 26. I was in my classroom when I found out I was one of the finalists. I went to the auditorium—I was very nervous. Then I was told that I had won. It was going to be announced over the P.A. to the whole school. I was very excited.

Next, I entered my invention in the state competition. I was at school when I found out that I was the fifth-grade winner for the state of Ohio, and I was going on to the regional Invent America! contest. I got to go to Greenfield Village in Dearborn, Michigan, because that's where the contest was held. I went there for a weekend with my family. I was excited and nervous. When we arrived in Dearborn, we checked into our hotel and then went to the Henry Ford Museum at Greenfield Village. I set up my invention in a booth so people could look at it and ask me questions. It was fun at Greenfield Village. I even met some new friends.

On the last day, the judges announced the winners from each grade. I didn't win. I was very disappointed, but happy that I had made it that far. Even though I didn't win the regional competition, I'm still getting the Ice Blades patented and am going to try to sell them. I learned that inventors never give up.

FUN INVENTIONS

Questions to Think About, Ideas to Try

1. Think of something important to you that is sometimes overlooked or forgotten. What could you invent to call attention to it?

2. Choose two or three children's toys or games. In what ways could you change them to make them more fun and exciting?

3. Ask your parents if you can go with them to work one day. While you're there, look around and see what goes on at their workplace. What things in their workplace could you improve or change to make them better? What could you play with and perhaps turn into an invention?

4. Product testing and research are important parts of the invention process. Make a list of the ways you'll test your invention. Then make a list of the places you'll contact or visit to research your invention.

5. Next time you play or watch a sporting event, look around at the equipment and the playing field. Watch how the participants play the game. What changes could you think of to make the game more efficient, safer, easier, or more fun?

6. Not all inventions have to make people's lives easier; some inventions make life more fun! What are some fun things you do that you could make more entertaining through your own invention?

7. Find out if there is an inventor's club at your school or in your community. If one doesn't exist, start one. An inventor's club could sponsor contests for getting students interested in the process of inventing. The club could also invite other students and adult inventors to speak to the student body.

HEALTH

Inventions

Lauren Patricia DeLuca

THE MEAL MARKER

Thirteen-year-old LAUREN PATRICIA DELUCA was born on May 4, 1981. She lives in Port Washington, New York, with her mom and dad, Susan and Larry, and her three sisters, Kristin, Karen, and Katie.

During her elementary years, Lauren attended the John Philip Sousa School. It was then that she had many first-place winners in the local Invention Conventions.

Lauren is now a student at Weber Junior High School. She is a member of the Port Enrichment Program, a class for gifted students. She plays the oboe in the school band, is a member of the volleyball and field hockey teams, and continues to involve herself in competitions in science and inventions.

She is also a member of her school's Science Olympiad Team, which won first place for the state of New York and went on to win third place in the national competition in Tucson, Arizona. Lauren's hobbies include sports, music, drawing, scuba diving, and hanging out with friends.

$\mathcal{I}$ SPEND A LOT OF TIME WITH MY SISTERS, ESPECIALLY my younger ones. I really enjoy doing things with them, so I try to come up with ways to entertain them. We have fun making and building doll houses and tents in the living room. One day, as I was making lunch for my sister and one of her friends, I decided to make faces on their oranges to make them more fun to eat. I found some

88

*Lauren
Patricia
DeLuca*

raisins, nuts, and other foods like that for the eyes, nose, and mouth. I held the food together with pieces of toothpicks that I had stuck into the orange. I thought decorating the food this way was a good idea, but my sister started complaining that small pieces of the toothpicks were in her orange.

It was then that I remembered an idea I had come up with when I was getting ready for my Halloween party. Before that party, I was trying to make eyeballs out of the grapes we were going to have with dinner. I couldn't think of any way to create the eyeballs other than writing on the grapes with a marker. That's when the idea first came to me: I would design a marker that contained food coloring instead of ink. That way, you could decorate your food and still be able to eat it.

Now that I had the idea again, the next step was to come up with a model. I talked to my mom about my idea and how I could make it. She gave me some of her dried-up refillable art markers. I took each one apart and removed the old tip. I also removed the inside cartridge, which holds the ink. I asked her if she had new parts to replace these. She said she didn't have all of them, only the new tips. I cleaned out a marker and put in one of the new tips. I still needed something to hold the food coloring inside the marker; I thought of using a paper towel. I took the paper towel and twisted it tightly until it looked like the cartridge that was originally inside the marker. I got out a bottle of blue food coloring and poured it into one end of the marker. I let the tip and the paper towel absorb all the coloring, and then I replaced the cap onto the end. Now I was ready to test my invention.

I found all different types of food to try my marker on, including fruit, bread, and vegetables. The marker worked well on hard, unwaxed surfaces. It even worked on sliced bread as long as you didn't press too hard. Even my younger sisters could use the marker. I made more markers in other colors so we would have a selection to use.

While we were having fun decorating the food, I did some brainstorming about a name or title for my markers. I wanted to come up with a clever title that would be self-explanatory. After awhile—and quite a few rejected names—I came up with "Meal Markers." The name seemed appropriate and also explained the invention at the same time.

Because I was using these markers as my entry into the local Invention Convention, I needed to do a bit of research for the product. I went to area art stores to see if anyone had food markers on the market. I didn't find anything like them, which helped convince me that I really did have a good idea. I also went to supermarkets and looked in the aisle where the stores sold icing and other food decorating supplies. I found plain food colorings, sprinkles, icing, gel for cakes, and other things similar to that, but I didn't find anything like my Meal Markers.

I entered my invention in our school's Invention Convention and won first place. From there, I entered the Meal Markers in the Invent America! state competition and won first place for the state of New York. For the regional competition, my teacher sent my invention information to the Invent America! judges. A few weeks later, I found out I had won first place.

While I was working on my invention, I kept a log of what I had done during the development of my project. I've done this for all my past inventions and have found it to be very helpful. Brainstorming in the beginning and during my project was very important. I was able to go back over my notes and create new ideas as I went along.

Lauren Patricia DeLuca (center) demonstrates her Meal Markers

I found it helpful to talk to my family and teachers about my ideas, too. Many times, I would get new ideas from them, or they might point out a possible problem. That's when it was time to rework my project or make an improvement.

I've learned many things in the past few years while I have been working on my inventions. One thing is that an invention does not have to be a huge new machine or something that will change the world. An invention may be an old idea with a new twist or improvement.

While you invent something, you are forced to think, plan, and solve a problem. At times this is easy, and at other times it is tiring. All of this thinking, planning, and solving teaches you to be persistent and patient. You also learn how to come up with an idea and to follow through to the end. Following through is one of the hardest things to do, especially when you are faced with a lot of problems.

One very important benefit that my inventions have given me, that I never considered until recently, is confidence in speaking to people and speaking in front of a group. During our local Invention Convention, I had to present my projects to judges, students, teachers, and friends. I had to learn to explain all the aspects of my designs clearly, and I needed to be prepared to answer any questions given to me. Now, when I work on inventions, science projects, or any other presentations, I no longer feel as scared or nervous in front of groups or judges as I did in the past.

I have not decided if I should get a patent for the Meal Markers yet. Getting a patent takes a lot of time and money and still doesn't guarantee someone else won't use your idea. A patent is still a possibility, though.

My suggestion to anyone thinking about inventing or designing something new is to first think about a problem that needs to be solved. Second, brainstorm and log any ideas on the solution. Third, come up with a plan and make some sketches if they are appropriate. Fourth, do research into similar products. Fifth, get working on the project; ask questions, answer them, and tie up loose ends. Sixth, have fun while you do it!

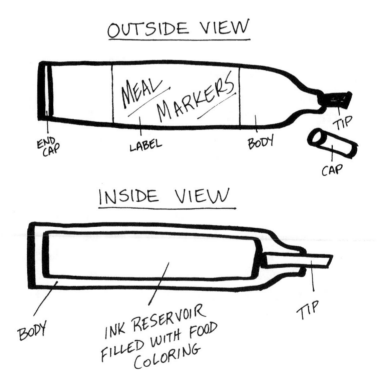

Lauren Patricia DeLuca's drawings of Meal Markers

THE ASTHMAMETER
AND MORE

JERI LEE is a seventeen-year-old junior at Hamilton High School in Hamilton, Texas. She has lived in this small central Texas community all of her life. Her father, Ralph, is self-employed, and her mother, Linda, teaches gifted students at the local school. Jeri has an older brother, Randy, and an older sister, Nancy.

Jeri's interests include reading, cross-stitching, and jewelry making. She is active in her church youth group, volleyball, band, golf, Students Against Driving Drunk (SADD), quiz bowl, the gifted program, cross country, and the flag corps. She participates in University Interscholastic League Calculator Applications and competed at the regional level during her freshman and sophomore years. She was selected for Who's Who Among American High School Students *in 1993 and 1994 and is a member of the National Honor Society. She plans to pursue her interests in inventing by majoring in engineering in college.*

$\mathcal{I}$ HAVE ALWAYS BEEN A PROBLEM-SOLVER, BUT I actually started inventing when I was in third grade. That year, I entered my school's invention contest and won first place with "The Feeder Keeper." That invention solved a problem I had with my dog. My dog liked to play with his bowl, and I would have to find it at feeding time. I drilled a hole in the bottom of the bowl and inserted a

Jeri Lee

long screw, which allowed me to attach the bowl into the ground. That way, the bowl stayed put, and I didn't have to go hunting to find it.

In fourth grade, I invented the "Handy Hair Bow Holder." I was always losing my hair bows and hair clips. I made a wooden stand and attached a magnet to it. This magnet held all my hair bows and hair clips and kept them from getting lost. I won third place with that invention.

In fifth grade, I invented "Freedom." That summer I had broken my arm, and I was upset because I couldn't go swimming and hot-tubbing with my parents and friends. To solve my problem, I invented a plastic mitt with an elastic armband to keep the water off the cast. "Freedom" brought me the first place award and also came in handy two years later when I again broke my arm.

In sixth grade, I invented the "Splash Guard." My mom would always fix blueberry muffins on Sunday morning. She would be all dressed up for church, and then she would open the blueberries and they would splash on her when the lid popped up. I cut a plastic bowl in half and attached it to the can opener so it would protect the person using the can opener from getting splashed.

In seventh grade, I won first place and Inventor of the Year in my school's invention contest with the "Blind Finder." I got my idea from having a friend who is visually impaired. I wondered how she knew where to go once she entered a store or building. The Blind Finder is a brass plate with Braille symbols on it, telling where the important areas are in the building. For example, it would include symbols for rest rooms, telephones, the front desk, stairs, elevators, and other important locations. The Blind Finder would be placed in a standard position to the left of the entrance to every public building. People who are visually impaired could use the Blind Finder and find their way around better without being so dependent on others. I am very proud of this idea because I believe that it could make the quality of life better for many people. I look forward to the day when this invention will be used in public places.

My eighth-grade year brought me to my last formal year of inventing, since it was the last year I could enter my school's contest. I spent a lot of time on this invention, so I have decided to describe in detail the steps I followed so that you, the reader (and future inventor), can see exactly how easy it is to invent.

The first step I took toward creating an invention was to brainstorm a list of all my problems. I suffer from mild to moderate asthma, and it bothers me especially during season changes, so I added this to my list. The next thing I did was to look at all of my problems on the list and think about how I might be able to solve each one.

When I got to the asthma problem, I thought, "Wouldn't it be great if I could know when I was going to have an asthma attack? That way, I could take preventive measures, such as avoiding what set off my asthma or taking my asthma medicine before an attack could develop." Then I thought, "What makes my asthma act up?" Some things that trigger my asthma are smoke, freshly cut grass, the smell of cedar and perfumes, and pollutants in the air. Of course, I knew that not all asthma sufferers have the same triggers, so I saved that problem to think about later.

My next thought was, "How could I know if those things were around me?" I could tell if smoke was around by a smoke detector, but that wouldn't help much. Besides, who wants to carry around a smoke detector all the time? I also knew that a smoke detector wouldn't help alert me to the other triggers, but a seed for an idea had been planted in my mind.

Jeri Lee with the display explaining her Asthmameter

My mind wouldn't let go of the smoke detector idea, so I looked up how a smoke detector works in *The Way Things Work* by David Macaulay (Houghton Mifflin, 1988), a book my brother had given me for Christmas. It explained that smoke detectors can sense the small particles of smoke that rise from a smoldering object and signal an alarm before a fire breaks out. "Hey," I thought, "that's what I need— something that can sense small particles of whatever triggers my asthma and then sends out an alarm before I start to have an asthma attack." The idea was beginning to come together. I read on.

The article said that ionizing detectors are electrical sensors that can detect smaller particles than those you can see. The ionizing smoke detector contains a chamber in which a low electric current flows through the air. Smoke particles entering the chamber increase its electrical resistance so that less current flows. A microchip responds to the drop in current by switching on an alarm. My next thought was, "If it can recognize smoke particles, why couldn't it recognize the other things that trigger asthma, since they, too, are airborne?"

I came to the conclusion that it could be done, and that the sensitivity could be set to accommodate different triggers in individual people. An interview with my family doctor was very helpful. I found out that the triggers of individual people can be identified by using allergy tests. He was generous with his time and answered all of my questions. Plus, he was extremely encouraging.

My next step was to do some more research on asthma. I went to the library at Tarleton State University in Stephenville, Texas, to find out as much as I could about this disease. What I found amazed me. I discovered that one out of eleven Americans has mild to severe asthma, and a large number of people die yearly as a result of this disease. Many children with asthma are restricted from certain activities and are constantly in and out of the hospital. They also miss a lot of school. These facts helped me show that my invention would be very useful.

To continue my research, which is an absolutely essential step in the inventing process, I interviewed the school nurse about asthma and the problems she had observed at school. She, too, was quite helpful. She gave me some pamphlets to read and some tapes to listen to. The pamphlets showed me exactly what happens during an asthma attack.

After collecting the needed information and checking to be certain that such a device didn't already exist, I planned my invention. It would work on the principle of an ionization chamber. When triggers went through the chamber, it would set off an alarm. This would alert me that I was around something that could cause me to have an asthma attack.

I named my invention the "Asthmameter." It would be about the size of a microchip so that it wouldn't be a burden to carry around or wear. I designed the sensor to be inside a necklace pendant for women, worn underneath a tie for men, on the underside of a watch for teenagers, inside a stuffed animal for babies and toddlers, or on button covers for anyone. With the sensor hidden in this way, it is less obvious and makes the person wearing it feel less self-conscious.

With this idea, I won first place and Inventor of the Year in our local Invention Convention. I was also the 1992 Invent America! winner for the state of Texas. Although my invention is not at a marketable stage right now, I hope to get a patent on it someday soon. However, even if that never occurs, I have the satisfaction of knowing that I can solve my own problems through inventing. That gives me a lot of confidence to face the future.

My advice to you is that there is a solution to every problem, so don't give up. Get busy. Every invention you come up with solves not only your problem but that same problem for others, too. Therefore, every time you invent you make the world a better place.

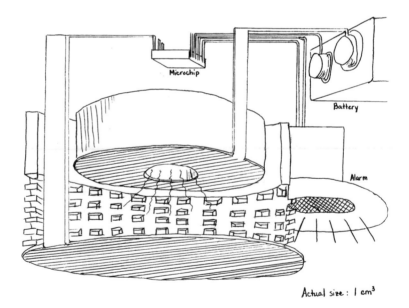

Jeri Lee's drawing of her Asthmameter

Laura Neubauer

NEUBIE'S NEBUWHIRL

Eleven-year-old LAURA NEUBAUER describes herself as "a friendly person with lots of freckles." She attends sixth-grade classes at Mitchell Middle School in Mitchell, South Dakota. Her favorite subjects are art and science. During the summer of 1993, her bas-relief print of a dancing buffalo, titled Seroon, *was on display at the South Dakota State Cultural Heritage Center in Pierre, South Dakota.*

Tap dancing and ballet classes, along with learning to play the guitar, keep Laura busy. When she has free time, she enjoys canoeing with her mom and dad, Kay and Joseph, and her sister, Bethany. She also enjoys playing softball, shooting baskets, and drawing original cartoons.

THE SKY LOOKS SUNNY AND STILL. I LEAN BACK IN my seat on the airplane with my stomach churning. I am anxious to see my mother and my sister, Bethany. I want to share with them all the interesting experiences I had at Greenfield Village in Dearborn, Michigan, showing visitors my invention, "Neubie's Nebuwhirl," and competing in the regional Invent America! contest.

The seed that my innovation grew from was planted when I was eight years old. That year, I was admitted to the hospital with micro plasma pneumonia. As part of my treatment, I had to take breathing therapy. That meant I inhaled a mist of medication. A machine called a *nebulizer* creates the mist by spinning air through a cup of medicine and turning the medicine into a mist. I have a lot of allergies, so my

Laura
Neubauer

doctor sent the nebulizer home with me so that I could continue with
my treatments three times a day.

I had trouble taking my treatments at home because I would get
bored breathing in and out of the machine. I would start reading a
book, watching television, or listening to a conversation and forget to
breathe through my mouth. My mom wasn't happy when she came into
the room and the medicine was evaporating into the room, not my
lungs. Neither of us knew that those tense moments would lead to three
months of brainstorming and inventing.

I found out about the Invent America! program when my sister,
Bethany, participated. When members of the medical auxiliary came to
school to talk about the program, I knew I wanted to invent something.
Everyone received a notebook that outlined the steps of inventing and
explained how to journal our ideas.

The Invent America! contest became the topic of conversation at
my family's dinner table every night. We shared ideas for projects and
thought up problems that bugged us. Then we tried to think of ways to
"debug" the problems. We discussed and trashed a lot of ideas before
I decided to try to improve the nebulizer.

I identified exactly what I wanted my invention to accomplish,
and I settled on three goals. First, I knew I wanted my invention to

make a noise when it was used properly. That way, even if I wasn't paying attention, my mom could hear if I was breathing the right way. Second, I needed to be able to disinfect the invention. Third, I wanted the invention to be inexpensive and made out of materials that were easy to locate.

The next step was to find something that would make a noise when I blew through it. The first possibility that came to my mind was a whistle. I went to the local discount stores and found plastic party favor whistles and party horns. The whistles made a good noise when you blew through them, but they didn't make a noise when you inhaled. After thinking about it for a while, I decided that inhaling was most important because I wanted to know when I was inhaling the medication.

I tried the party horns, and they made noise when I inhaled and exhaled. Part of the party horns, however, were made of paper. I could not disinfect the paper with the vinegar solution I wanted to use. I decided to keep looking. It was important to me that my invention meet all three of my goals.

The search continued for about three weeks. I was starting to worry that I might have to find someone to make a part for me. I wanted to stay away from that if I could, because of the cost. I asked my whole family to keep their eyes open for anything that makes noise. One day, our dedication paid off. My mom was doing her regular grocery shopping and decided to look in the party section. She found a party toy that consisted of a plastic fan-style whizzer in the opening of a balloon.

As a toy, it wasn't much fun, but the whizzer was perfect for my invention; it met all three of my goals. First, it made a whizzing noise both when I inhaled and exhaled. (If I inhaled and held my breath until the fan stopped, I would know I was not breathing too quickly.) Second, it was made of plastic so I could disinfect it. Third, it was inexpensive. The whizzer also snapped snugly into the nebulizer's tube; I didn't need to make any changes to it. Eureka!

The next step was taking my invention to experts to see if there was anything like it on the market. I went to the local hospital and asked the person in charge of respiratory therapy to look at my invention. He examined it and said that there were other products that whistled when you were breathing too fast, but none that made a noise to remind you to inhale. He asked me a lot of questions, and said he thought my idea was a good one.

My last task was to name my invention. I came up with about ten names and then chose "Neubie's Nebuwhirl," because my nickname is Neubie and Nebuwhirl describes what it does. I also realized what I had wasn't an invention because nothing I used was new. I had an

Laura Neubauer (r) demonstrates her Nebuwhirl

innovation. I had taken two products that already existed and put them together to improve a product.

I entered Neubie's Nebuwhirl in the school district's invention competition, and I won. Next, my teacher sent information about my invention to the Invent America! judges. They wrote back, telling me I was the fourth-grade winner for the state of South Dakota. That's when my dad and I got to travel to Dearborn for the regional competition.

Flying home from Michigan, I thought about how happy I was that I had won the Invent America! contest for my state. I had a lot of fun and I enjoyed seeing Thomas Edison's laboratory at Greenfield Village and seeing all of the other kids' inventions. Most of all, I'm glad I participated because I learned that I can solve problems that affect people like me.

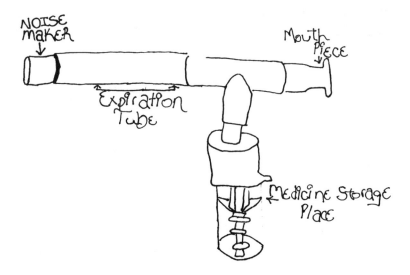

Laura Neubauer's drawing of Neubie's Nebuwhirl

HEALTH INVENTIONS

Questions to Think About, Ideas to Try

1. Jeri Lee's Asthmameter detects air pollutants that cause her asthma to act up. In a way, her invention detects problems. What other types of inventions could help detect problems in your home, school, or community?

2. Some people who have medical problems require special machines and facilities to help them live normal lives. Pay attention to people who are physically challenged. How could you make their lives easier? Think of a new machine or an improvement of one that already exists.

3. Consider some of the health problems facing people today: allergies, epilepsy, arthritis, muscular dystrophy, multiple sclerosis, spina bifida, visual impairment, hearing impairment, cystic fibrosis, AIDS, cancer, hemophilia, and cerebral palsy, among others. Find out what daily activities people with one or more of these health problems find difficult to handle. What could you invent that would make life easier for people with one or more of these problems?

4. Brainstorm a list of names for an invention you've been thinking about. Write down every idea; fill the page. When you're done, read through your list and circle your favorites. You'll find more ideas for naming your invention in Part Two of this book.

5. Many young inventors have used the book, *The Way Things Work*, by David Macaulay as a resource. If you haven't already read it, you can find a copy of it at your local library or bookstore. You can also find it on CD-ROM. This resource may jump-start your brain into the invention process.

Safety Inventions

Katya Harfmann

TIPPER TOES

Nine-year-old KATYA HARFMANN lives in Butlerville, Ohio, a small rural community outside of Cincinnati. A fourth-grader at Harlan-Butlerville Elementary, she is an honors student and enjoys her time at school. Her favorite subjects are math and science. Katya lives on a ten-acre farm with her mom and dad, Janina and Anton, and her older sister, Kristen. The farm is also home to the family's dog, two cats, and ten chickens.

During the week, Katya is active with swim team practices, Girl Scouts, school projects, and church activities. In what little free time she has, Katya likes to read, spend time with and care for her animals, and play games with her family. She has been an inventor for three years.

ONE OF MY FAVORITE TV SHOWS IS "RESCUE 911." I love to watch people helping other people and figuring out ways to stay safe. One night while I was watching, I noticed a problem that I thought I could fix. On the show, a young girl had tipped the kitchen chair she was sitting on and had fallen over backwards. She was seriously injured and rushed to the hospital. I see many kids in school tip their chairs back, too. My teacher tells them to stop, but they keep doing it. They think tipping the chair is fun, but it really could be dangerous. Chairs that have straight-back legs are big problems for young children. They can tip back easily.

Katya
Harfmann

I decided to invent something that would prevent chairs from tipping over backwards. People with young children could put my invention on a regular chair to make it childproof.

I came up with a foot that attaches to the back of each chair leg. A screw attaches the foot, called the "Tipper Toe," to the bottom of the chair leg. The foot is shaped like a triangle and sticks out of the back of the chair leg. The chair can't tip back because the foot holds the chair straight.

Inventing Tipper Toes was hard work, but it was also a lot of fun. After I had my idea, I started out by doing my research at our local public library. In a book about safety, I found a list of addresses to write to for more help. I wrote lots of letters to see if there was already an invention like mine. Most of the people I wrote to were very friendly and wrote back. People told me that falling accidents are very bad for children. Also, no one had ever heard of any way to prevent chairs from tipping.

My next step was to start my experiments. This part was the most fun for me, because I always like to try to make things. To make a model of my invention, I used simple things we had around the house: tape, rulers, and clay. I taped the ruler to the back leg of the chair so that it stuck out like a foot.

I didn't know how long the foot needed to be to stop the chair from tipping, so I tried it at different lengths. Some were too short and some were too long. It felt really good when I finally found the length that worked. Then I used hunks of clay to make the foot the shape I wanted it to be. It was easy to use the clay, and I could do it by myself, because it wasn't dangerous. If I made a mistake, I just smushed the clay together and started again until it looked right.

When the shape was the way I wanted it, I knew I needed to make a stiffer model so that I could test the invention. I gave the clay model to my dad, and he copied the shape onto a piece of wood. I helped with the sanding and painting. That was fun, too. For the test, I attached the wooden model to a chair and found that it was very hard to tip the chair backwards. My invention worked.

Next, I drew pictures of my invention. These pictures had to look very nice and neat so people would be able to understand them. I drew them over and over. It was hard to get them right, but I kept trying because they were important. Sometimes I felt like crying or ripping the paper up! Now when I look at my drawings, I am proud of them because I took the time to make them right.

To name my invention, I started by making a list of words that meant the same as "chair," "foot," "tip," and "safe." I put the words together in lots of different ways. Some combinations sounded really silly. Some were like tongue-twisters. I thought Tipper Toes sounded the best.

Because I was the only student at my school who had invented something, my mom and I submitted Tipper Toes to the state competition. A few weeks later, while I was in school, my mom received a letter from the Invent America! judges. The letter said I was the winner for the state of Ohio. My mom drove to my school and told me the news. I felt great.

I displayed my invention at the regional Invent America! convention at the Henry Ford Museum at Greenfield Village in Dearborn, Michigan. That was really exciting! At first, I was nervous about talking to people I didn't know, but everyone was very nice. I met a lot of other young inventors from other states and learned how some famous inventors got started. Unfortunately, I didn't place at that competition.

At home, people who know about my invention still ask me about it. Most people say, "That's a really good idea. You should sell it." I have saved all of my notes, drawings, and the model in case I decide to

Katya Harfmann (l) with her Tipper Toes Display

sell it someday. That way, people will know it is really my idea. I would like to see my invention patented and eventually sold in stores so every family could buy the Tipper Toes. During my research, I looked in many stores for an invention like mine. I didn't find any, but some stores said they would sell it if I made it. Maybe someday I will.

If I did make and sell my invention, I would choose to make it out of nylon or hard plastic because those materials won't break easily or scratch floors, and because regular chair feet are made out of these materials. I think a factory that works with plastic would be able to easily make my invention, because it is all one piece.

I learned a lot from my project, and I got a chance to try many new things I had never done before. I've gotten pretty good at using a computer after writing all those letters to people. I was able to make and build things. I had a lot of practice drawing, too. I've learned where to go for help and not to be afraid to talk to people about my ideas. The people I've met have been really nice and encouraged me to keep inventing.

I would encourage other kids to invent things, too. There are many things that could be made better. Your idea might not work right the first time, but don't give up. If you keep trying and do things a different way, you can make something really neat.

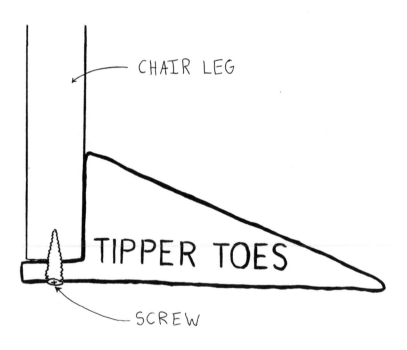

Katya Harfmann's drawing of her Tipper Toes

Sarita M. James

COMPUTERS AND SPEECH RECOGNITION

SARITA M. JAMES, 18, was born in Brooklyn, New York, in 1976. Her family later moved to Chillicothe, Ohio, and then to Fort Wayne, Indiana. Her parents, Dr. T. D. James and Dr. Pushpom James, have their medical practices in Fort Wayne. As a senior at Homestead High School, Sarita ranked first in her class of over 350 students.

During the 1993–1994 school year, she was a co-president of the speech team, vice-president of her chapter's Junior Classical League (an organization devoted to the study of the ancient Romans and the Latin language), and senior representative of Homestead's Key Club, a service organization.

Along with her older brother, Rajesh, Sarita is now an undergraduate at Harvard University. She has played the piano since she was four years old and has entered several competitions. Her hobbies include doing jigsaw puzzles and playing chess. She also enjoys walking in the woods behind her home, where she has friends among the local deer population.

$\mathcal{I}$'VE BEEN COMPETING IN SCIENCE FAIR PROJECTS since first grade. Whether the subject was earthworms, the structure of fats, or cloning animals or plants, I was always researching something. When I was in high school, I became interested in computer *neural networks*—and that led me to my invention: a computer that could easily recognize a person's voice.

While I was in high school, I heard a talk given by Dr. Samir Sayegh, a professor at Purdue University in Indiana. The talk was about neural networks. Using computers, researchers set up neural networks to imitate the way a human brain thinks. Though Dr. Sayegh's talk was interesting, I did not know very much about neural networks. I decided to take college courses so that I could learn more. Even though I was still in high school, I became a full-time college student. I took graduate-level courses about neural networks. By my senior year in high school, I had finally learned the math and computer languages needed to do some work with neural networks.

I wanted to use what I had learned to find a way for computers to easily recognize what people are saying. In reading scientific journals, I found that most computer systems have a hard time understanding people's speech. Background noise, continuous speech (little or no pause between words), and many people talking at once distract the computer.

For my invention, I decided to work with computers that are on helicopters. A helicopter is an excellent example of a place where background noise can be a big problem to a computer. I wanted to teach the computer to understand speech in spite of the background noise. That way, a helicopter pilot could use voice commands to fly the helicopter. The pilot's hands could be free to do other work.

Making a system that would understand a person's voice was a time-consuming job. Along with using neural networks, I used another computer tool called a *wavelet*. The wavelet made it easier for my neural networks to understand the sounds they heard.

Sarita M.
James

My system used phonemic analysis to recognize words. *Phonemes* are distinct vocal sounds, such as the long and short "i" and the "ch" sounds. In phonemic analysis, words are broken down into individual sounds. Phonemic analysis makes a computer system more powerful than other systems because all words can be described as groupings of sounds. A system that uses phonemic analysis can recognize any word in any language, as long as the programmer tells the computer how each word sounds.

Once I assembled my system, my first objective was to train the neural network to recognize all of the phonemes (there are between forty-one and forty-five in General American English). I trained the neural networks by adding helicopter background noise and applying wavelets to half of the phoneme samples. I wrote computer programs, which were based on the work done by scientists in the European community, to teach the neural network to recognize these sounds.

After my neural network knew all the phonemes, I rebuilt my system so that it could recognize words based on the phonemes it had heard. After many, many revisions, my system was able to recognize nearly every word it heard.

I created a display board and wrote a paper detailing my research. I wanted other people to understand the basic ideas behind my project.

I was in my high school's ALPHA Mentorship program, which links students with professionals in the community. With my helpful ALPHA Mentorship Coordinator Jan Viars, I traveled during the school year with my invention to compete in national and international science competitions.

In the spring of 1994, at the 45th Annual International Science and Engineering Fair, I was lucky enough to be named one of two students to share the top award, informally called the "Student Nobel Prize." The award included an all-expenses-paid trip to Stockholm, Sweden, for the Nobel Prize ceremonies. I was ecstatic because this had really been my dream award.

Sarita M. James (r) explains her speech recognition invention

In December, I traveled to Sweden. The trip was all a fairy tale. The King of Sweden took the time to meet me and talk to me at the Royal Palace. I also heard the lectures of the adult Nobel Prize winners, and became friends with many of them at the parties and functions that the Nobel Foundation arranged. On the last day I was there, the Nobel Foundation held a grand banquet and ball. The foundation had kindly paid for dancing lessons for me (which I really needed), so I danced the night away. That trip was the most exciting two weeks of my life.

I have met many remarkable people through science competitions, and, due to the generosity of many organizations, I have been able to pay for a good part of my college education. I've also been featured in newspapers and magazines, such as *Time, USA Today* (in its feature on the country's top twenty students), *Fortune, Business Week, Forbes*, and *Science News*.

Through my work in science, I have found that being curious really helps. If you want to discover something new, try to find a problem to solve and then learn as much as you can about the problem. You may think of a new way to solve the problem—but do not be disappointed if it takes a long time for your solution to work. Remember to always think for yourself and listen to your ideas, even if they sound crazy at first. For me, it all started with those experiments about earthworms, the structures of fats, and cloning from my elementary and middle school years.

THE KIDDIE STOOL

Thirteen-year-old JEANIE LOW is a seventh-grader at Paul Revere School in Houston, Texas. She is an honors student and has all E's in conduct. She is interested in school activities such as playing the trombone.

Her father, Richard, is a pediatrician and her mother, Susan, is an office manager. Jeanie has a younger sister, Elizabeth, who is also an inventor, and two other siblings, William and Christensen.

Jeanie enjoys inventing and also finds time to have fun with her family and her friends. She likes horseback riding, ice skating, and playing with her pets. At school, Jeanie enjoys science. She hopes to become an archaeologist or an inventor.

*M*Y INVENTING ACTIVITIES ALL STARTED IN kindergarten, when I entered an invention fair at school. For the fair, I invented the "Kiddie Stool" because my dad would always break the plastic step-stools in the bathroom. The plastic stools would get in the way and there was no place to store them in our small bathroom.

The Kiddie Stool is unlike other stools. It is a folding stool that connects to a cabinet; you can fold it up or down for easy access. You can even move it out of the way. When it is not in use, you can easily fold the stool against the door of the vanity cabinet so adults can reach the sink without stumbling on it. The Kiddie Stool connects to any cabinet in any room in your house, from the bathroom to the kitchen. You can easily assemble the stool; it really doesn't take much time to

116

place it where little kids need it. My invention was quite useful, especially for my little sister who could not reach the sink.

To make the Kiddie Stool, I first tied wires to hold the stool step to the cabinet door. I decided that would not work because I thought smaller children might choke or cut themselves on the wire. After awhile, I decided to use magnets to hold the stool parts up against the cabinet. Then I went to a hardware store to get some wood. I also bought magnets, hinges, screws, nails, and some other hardware materials. I went to the wood department and asked the salespeople to cut some wood for me. They happily did this. As they were cutting the wood, they asked me what was I making. I told them about my invention and the salespeople said the stool could not be made. I proved them wrong, however, because my invention definitely works.

I entered my Kiddie Stool in the invention fair at my school. I placed first and was quite surprised.

A few years later, when I was seven years old, my family and I heard about the First Annual Invention Fair that was being held at a mall in Houston. I entered the Kiddie Stool and won first place at that fair. When I got home and turned on the TV, I saw myself on the news, showing my invention.

After that, I appeared on the TV show, "Good Morning Houston." Since then, I have also appeared twice in the *Houston Post*

Jeanie Low

newspaper demonstrating my Kiddie Stool. I have also addressed the Houston Chamber of Commerce and the Texas Creative Society.

A few years ago, my family and I found out about the Houston Inventors Association, a club for inventors. We decided to join and about a week later we went to the first meeting. Two meetings later, I talked to the other members about what they thought of my invention. After that, I talked to the chairman and the president of the society. We had a good talk about the meeting and about how the members could help me get publicity and some perspectives from people older and younger than me. Now, I go to the monthly meetings, find out how other people are doing with their inventions, and learn about current things that are happening to inventions in the marketplace.

One of the club members is a patent attorney. He has helped me get my patent. First, we drew diagrams of the Kiddie Stool. Then we tried to think of ways to improve the Kiddie Stool, but we stuck with

Jeanie Low demonstrates her Kiddie Stool

the basic design. I developed the pre-packaged Kiddie Stool Kit, which contained the hardware, precut wood, and decorations for the stool. The stool came ready to be attached with screws to any cabinet door.

After we looked for ways to improve my invention, we did some research and discovered that, so far, I am the only person in the world to have a folding stool like this. I decided to apply for a patent. The patent attorney told me not to be upset if my patent didn't come through; but, believe it or not, my patent came through on the first try. Most inventions take more than one try for the patent to come through. It can take up to seventeen tries for such a thing to happen. So you see why I was so happy when I got my patent.

During the summer of 1993, my family and I went to Washington, D.C. The people at the Patent Office had invited me to display the Kiddie Stool at the Smithsonian Institution. When they invited me, they didn't realize I was a kid. All they knew was that I had a patent and that my invention was good. Many people and corporations were invited to exhibit their inventions, but I was the only kid there. Over 10,000 people came to see my invention. I met with patent officials and even attended Washington's first-ever invention society meeting. I also met some government officials and teachers from Brazil. I gave them handouts on my inventions and the invention society. I also talked to them about how to get kids in Brazil interested in inventing. During the show, a reporter from *Inventors' Digest* magazine interviewed me.

My sister, Elizabeth, is also an inventor.* In October, 1993, I went to California with my family, where my sister and I went to film a TV show called "Why Didn't I Think of That?" The show aired on November 6, 1993. The TV crew was really nice to me and my family. At first, taping was pretty easy, but it got harder as we went along. Being on a TV show is really fun. You get to see what it is like to be on a show and also what goes on behind the scenes.

I have begun marketing the Kiddie Stool to various companies and am working on a pamphlet and a videotape to describe it. I went to the Inventing New Products Exposition (INPEX) in Pittsburgh,

---

* Elizabeth Low's story appears on pages 75–80.

Pennsylvania, in May, 1994. That show is the largest invention fair in the world; over thirty countries were represented, including China and Russia. I won a gold medal in that competition, against adults from all of those countries. I was also asked to appear in *Cobblestone* and *Woman's Day* magazines.

Since the Kiddie Stool, I have also invented an alarm for the bathtub. The alarm would go off when the tub starts to overflow or if a small child is drowning. I also invented a circular doormat with spinning brushes. Another invention I thought of uses cushioning material on doorknobs for people with arthritis. The material makes the doorknobs easier to grab.

I enjoy inventing, and I like to find solutions to problems in my life and in other peoples' lives. I want to try to help when I am needed. I have displayed things at invention meetings and talked with other kids and teachers about how to develop their inventions. Teachers have asked me to talk to their classes on how to invent successfully.

If anyone is thinking about making an invention or becoming an inventor, they should always pursue their ideas and thus experience the joys of discovering new inventions. I am really happy about what I have accomplished with my life so far and am especially happy with my Kiddie Stool invention.

I love to talk to other kids about how to improve their inventions. When I do, I give them a copy of the "Top Ten List for a Successful Invention," which my sister and I developed. I suggest that they review the list to see if their invention is marketable.

JEANIE AND ELIZABETH LOW'S TOP TEN LIST FOR A SUCCESSFUL INVENTION

10. The invention must either fulfill a need, simplify a task, or fill a void. If there is not a good market for the product, it will not succeed.

9. Keep it simple. Do not reinvent the entire wheel; rather, modify a small part of it.

8. Concentrate on a particular inventing area; something you are familiar with, such as things around your house, at school, or ideas for toys. Then focus on a more limited area. (In the Low family, Jeanie works on inventions for the bathroom; Elizabeth works on things for the office.)

7. Do the research and testing. Come up with the best product possible.

6. Give the invention a catchy name. The best idea can be unmarketable if the name does not instantly convey what the product does or what it is. Also, the name must be easy to pronounce and remember.

5. Ask for advice from others if there is no invention society in your community.

4. Make the product colorful and durable. If it is brightly packaged, it will catch the buyer's eye. If it breaks right away, people will not buy it.

3. Make a model that demonstrates how your product works. Even a scale model will still give people the idea.

2. Learn all you can about the product's use in society and talk with enthusiasm when describing it.

And our number one hint (drum roll):

1. Have fun with your invention.

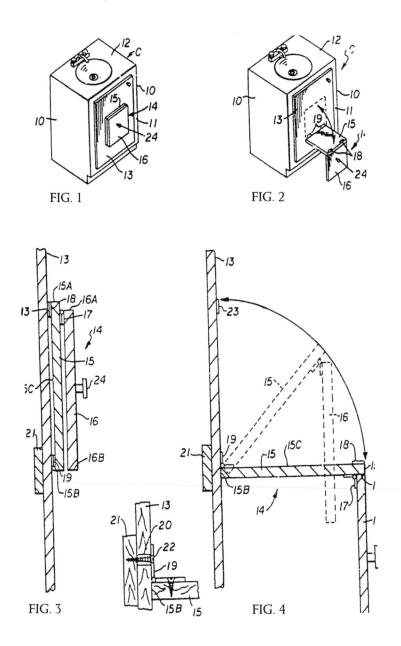

FIG. 1

FIG. 2

FIG. 3

FIG. 4

Patent drawings of Jeanie Low's Kiddie Stool

SAFETY INVENTIONS

Questions to Think About, Ideas to Try

1. Make a list of people who might help you take your invention idea from paper to model.

2. With input from friends and family, make a list of safety concerns that affect children, young people, and adults. Pick one and think of an invention that would address the problem.

3. What parts of the computer would you like to change? Would you change the way the music sounds on games or the shape of the keyboard? Start your inventing process by thinking of changes you'd like to make.

4. Invent a computer program that would help young students with schoolwork in an area that interests you, such as writing, reading, math, social studies, or science.

5. Take a piece of paper and a pen and walk through your home. Write down anything you notice that you would like to change to make your life safer or easier. Make a list of ideas for each room in your home. Don't forget the garage!

PART TWO

How to Be an Inventor

GET STARTED

$\mathcal{N}$OW THAT YOU'VE READ ABOUT THE GIRLS AND young women and their inventions, you may be thinking that you'd like to be an inventor. Maybe you already have an idea you'd like to try. Or maybe you need to come up with an idea. It doesn't matter what stage you're at—if you want to become an inventor, you're already on your way.

What can inventing do for you? Here are just a few of the benefits it offers:

- Inventing helps you to think more creatively.
- It opens the door to a world of problem solving, imagination, and innovation.
- It sharpens your scientific skills as you observe, collect data, organize, generalize, predict, and revise.
- It builds your research skills.
- It gives you a chance to play with ideas that interest you.
- It provides you with challenge and excitement.
- It enables you to make a real contribution to the world.
- It helps you to gain confidence in your own abilities as you become a more creative and productive person.
- It puts you in touch with interesting people.
- It exposes you to new ideas and information.
- It may even point you toward a possible career or life direction.

How can you get started being an inventor? Where should you begin?

The first step is very simple: Get a notebook. It doesn't have to be expensive or fancy; a plain spiral notebook will work just fine. You'll use your notebook to collect, organize, and record your thoughts and the information you gather. It will be your Inventor's Notebook. Keep your Inventor's Notebook with you all the time. Carry it in your backpack to school. Put it next to your bed at night. You'll want to have your Inventor's Notebook near you whenever you come up with an interesting thought, idea, or question related to inventing.

Next, find a place where you can think, store the materials you gather, experiment, and invent. If possible, this should be a place where you can work undisturbed for periods of time. Depending on what you are inventing, you might be able to work in your room. Or you might need a corner of the garage or workroom in your basement. Or maybe there is a place at school you can call your own for a few hours during the week. Check with your parents and teachers. Explain that you'll need a place to work on your inventions.

What now? You need an idea!

COME UP WITH IDEAS

Every invention begins as an idea in someone's mind. The pencil, the stapler, Post-it notes, computers, cars, Kleenex, lightbulbs, water faucets, ceiling tiles, window blinds, paper clips, shoelaces...all started out as ideas.

Ideas for inventions are all around you. You simply need to look *differently* at everyday objects, activities, and problems. Let your mind explore new possibilities and fresh solutions. What hasn't been thought of yet? What hasn't been tried? What hasn't been discovered? Try not to limit your thinking in any way. Sometimes the wildest, silliest, most off-the-wall ideas can lead to useful, practical inventions.

Try this: In your Inventor's Notebook, keep track of your activities for one whole 24-hour day. Record everything you do from the moment you get up in the morning until you get up the following morning. Then review your notes. Was there anything that bothered you? Anything that annoyed you? Anything you wish had been simpler, easier, more fun to do? Write down your thoughts in your Inventor's

Notebook. Then brainstorm solutions—any solutions you can think of. Again, try not to limit your thinking in any way.

Don't get caught in the "I-Can't-Do-It" trap. If you find yourself thinking "I'm too young," or "I could never do this," or "I'm just a girl," or "I don't have enough money to do this," or "This is a silly idea," or "No one would want this," or "This won't work," STOP and return to the process later. Take a break, get some fresh air, or think about something else for a while. Return to your brainstorming at another time.

You might want to ask your family and friends to help you with this process, because the more ideas you collect and combine, the more likely you will end up with creative ideas of high quality. As the American poet Oliver Wendell Holmes once said, "Many ideas grow better when transplanted into another mind than in the one where they spring up." Try "transplanting" someone else's idea into your mind and see what happens. Take a new slant, a different interpretation. Ask questions that lead you to new conclusions.

Try this: Survey your parents, siblings, relatives, neighbors, friends, teachers, and others about things they would like to see invented or changed. Use these statements to guide you as you gather ideas from others:

▶ "I wish I had a better way of _____."

▶ "The things that bother me most about my daily activities are _____."

▶ "The products I would like to see improved are _____."

▶ "My life would be easier if _____."

▶ "I am often inconvenienced by _____."

Record their responses in your Inventor's Notebook. Later, read through them and write down any ideas for inventions that come to mind. The more ideas you have to choose from, the more likely you are to come up with one or more successful inventions.

CHOOSE AN IDEA TO PURSUE

Now that you've got a list of ideas and possible solutions, it's time to identify one (or more) you want to try to turn into inventions. At this point in the invention process, you're still thinking about ideas—don't worry yet about how you'll build something or how a product will work. Concentrate on the possibilities. Ask yourself, "Which idea appeals the most to me?"

Many of the girls and young women in this book wrote about how hard it was to come up with an idea for an invention. Many of them thought about everyday problems and how they could solve them. Melissa Jo Buck saw the problems her mother had in cleaning the kitchen floor. Emma Tillman thought about the problems she had in draining the water from her family's pool. At first, these inventors didn't think about the actual end product. They just came up with an idea to solve a problem.

Once you've chosen an idea, do some preliminary research on whether your idea already exists as an invention. As Jamie Lynn Villella was developing her E. Z. Vac idea, she wrote to some doctors and to the Arthritis Foundation, asking for their feedback. Laura Neubauer asked the person in charge of respiratory therapy at a local hospital if he had seen anything like her invention, Neubie's Nebuwhirl.

Try this: Read through the ideas you've gathered in your Inventor's Notebook. Decide which idea you'd like to pursue further. Complete some preliminary research on that idea. If your idea already exists as an invention, pick another idea and research that one. If your idea doesn't already exist as an invention, you're ready for the next step: turning your idea into an invention.

TURN YOUR IDEA INTO AN INVENTION

Once you have an idea for an invention, you also have a "problem": figuring out how to turn your idea into an invention. The creative problem-solving process developed by Sidney Parnes and Alex Osborn will help you with this next step in the invention process. The problem-solving process begins with identifying the problem, or in the case of inventing, identifying the idea, which you did in the "Choosing an Idea to Pursue" section.

The next five stages are Fact-Finding, Problem-Finding, Idea-Finding, Solution-Finding, and Acceptance-Finding. During each stage, be sure to give yourself some "incubation time"—time to pause, reflect, and think some more. Incubation frees your mind for new ideas and creative possibilities. Use your Inventor's Notebook to keep a record of the fresh mental images that come to you along the way.

FACT-FINDING

In fact-finding, you list facts and clarify your idea by asking yourself questions that begin with *who, what, where, when, why,* and *how*.

Before Stefanie Lynn Garry made her Adjustable Broom, she looked at *who* would be using the broom (people of different ages and different heights) and *how* they would use it (to sweep under tables and clean cobwebs off the ceiling). Meghan Hatfield identified *why* she should develop the Driver's License Number Scanner (so information about someone could be found easily and quickly).

Try this: In your Inventor's Notebook, think about your idea and write down your own *who, what, where, when, why,* and *how* questions. Leave enough space between each question to write in your answers.

PROBLEM-FINDING

Now, look at your idea in different ways using questions that begin with "In What Way Might...?"

Jeri Lee asked herself many of these questions before she invented the Asthmameter: "In what way might I know that an asthma attack is coming?," "In what way might I find out what makes my asthma act up?," "In what way might I alert myself that asthma triggers are nearby?"

Try this: In your Inventor's Notebook, write down three or four of your own "In What Way Might...?" questions.

IDEA-FINDING

In the idea-finding stage, you read through your list of "In What Way Might...?" questions and select the one that interests you the most. Then you brainstorm a list of solutions.

Jeri Lee was most interested in knowing when asthma triggers were nearby. Her list of solutions included finding a device that could sense particles in the air.

Try this: Look over your "In What Way Might...?" questions. Circle the one that you are most interested in. On a new sheet of paper, make a list of ways you could answer that question.

SOLUTION-FINDING

After listing all possible solutions, you're ready to determine which one will work best. One way to find the best solution is to use a decision-making grid. The grid contains your list of solutions and a list of questions. You rank each solution from 1 to 5, according to how favorably it answers the question (5 is most favorable; 1 is least favorable). Add up the numbers and the solution with the highest total is the most favorable.

Try this: Create your own decision-making grid. Along the left side of a piece of paper, list all the solutions you came up with in the idea-finding stage. Across the top of the page, write down questions to help you evaluate these solutions. The questions could include:

▶ "Which solution will have the most lasting benefits?"

▶ "Which will be the easiest to implement?"

▶ "Which will cost the least to implement?"

▶ "Which will have the greatest potential for positive results?"

▶ "Which will be the most environmentally safe?"

Look at your first solution and the first question. Put a number by that solution, depending on how well it answers the question. Continue reading solutions and questions until you've ranked all of your solutions. Now, add up the numbers across one line. The solution with the largest total is the most favorable.

ACCEPTANCE-FINDING

In the acceptance-finding stage, you prepare a plan to put your most favorable solution—your invention solution—to work. At this stage, you determine what equipment and help you'll need, and a timeline for what is to be done first, second, and so on.

Try this: At the top of a page in your Inventor's Notebook, write down the invention idea you determined to be the most favorable. Make a list of equipment you'll need. Where will you go to get this equipment? List people you could ask for help if you need it. What part of your invention will you design first? What will be next? How will you test your invention?

DEVELOP A SKETCH

Once you've identified an idea and determined an invention solution, you're ready to draw your invention. Even if you don't think of yourself as an artist, don't skip this stage of the inventing process. The purpose of your sketch is to get your idea into a picture format. You may have your invention planned perfectly in your mind, but in order to convey your idea to other people, you must get that image onto paper.

Use the pages in your Inventor's Notebook to draw your invention in several different ways—big or small, long or short, with or without certain features. Use a pencil so that you can erase and modify your sketches, but be sure to put the date next to each drawing. And remember, these sketches aren't for an art show; they're for you to use in clarifying your ideas to yourself and others.

PUT IT ALL TOGETHER

With your completed sketches, you're ready to create a *model* of your invention. As Katina Stewart, Katya Harfmann, and other inventors found out, making a model usually requires the help of an adult. Show your sketches to your parents, teachers, or other adult. Tell them your ideas for how to build your invention. Can they help you choose the right materials, as Katina's mom did for Katina's Clothes Saver? Can they help you build the model, as Katya's dad did for the Tipper Toes invention?

Look at the equipment list and plan of action that you created in the acceptance-finding stage described above. Assemble all the materials you'll need in one place. Look at the people you listed as resources. How can they help you build your model?

As you develop the model, consider the people who will use your invention, and consider how they will use it. Will your invention need to be child-proof? Will it need to be larger or smaller? If someone must turn on your invention, where will the switch be located?

Keep working at your model. Experiment with different materials. And don't be afraid to make modifications or changes to your original invention design. Before inventing Ice Blades, Emily Tucker tried many different combinations of bolts and wheels. For the Vacuum Dirt Mat, Jennifer Garcia tried different switch settings to activate her invention.

Once you're satisfied with your model, you can build a *prototype*. The difference between a model and a prototype is that the prototype is an exact duplicate of the finished invention in every way—from size and shape to materials and color. After Emily Tucker had decided upon a wheel and bolt combination, she built a prototype of her Ice Blades. She used her prototype to test out the strength of the bolts.

GIVE IT A NAME

The name you give your product will influence the way other people feel about buying it. The name actually helps to sell the invention, so create as much appeal as possible in the name. The name can also help people to understand and remember your invention.

Try this: Take your Inventor's Notebook with you as you tour local department, hardware, and specialty stores. Examine products similar to your invention. Read product names and write down the ones that appeal to you. Write down the ones you don't like on another page. Survey your family and friends for their opinions on product names that they like. Write those names in your notebook, too. Read through your lists and determine any pattern in the names you like and dislike.

Some products are named after the inventor, while others use the components or some special feature of the invention. You might try developing an acronym for your product. An *acronym* is a word formed from the initial letters of other words. For example, "scuba" is the acronym for Self-Contained Underwater Breathing Apparatus. The simple word "scuba" sounds more appealing—and is easier to say and remember—than the longer name. Try not to get too wordy with your product name.

Another idea for naming your product is to use a word origins or etymology book to help generate ideas. Or use a dictionary to analyze various combinations of prefixes and suffixes.

Try this: In your Inventor's Notebook, write a description of your product, including how it works and why it's needed. Circle all the major words in the description. Put these words and their synonyms on another piece of paper. Make several different combinations of these words to create your product name.

Never underestimate the value of a name. To determine the value of the name you've chosen, ask yourself the following questions.

▶ "Does the name sound interesting or appealing?"

▶ "Is the name easy to remember?"

▶ "Does the name help others understand the product?"

▶ "Will the name help to sell the product?"

Once you've decided on a name, the next step is to find out if anyone else has already used that name. To help you with this process, talk to a librarian. He or she can help you locate the nearest Patent and Trademark Depository Library (PTDL). Most PTDLs are located at the main library in your state capital. Through systems such as microfilm, microfiche, and CD-ROM, you can conduct your own patent and name search.

For more information on researching your name, order the booklet, "Basic Facts about Registering a Trademark," from the U.S. Government Printing Office. (They charge a fee for this booklet.) Write to:

U.S. Government Printing Office
Superintendent of Documents
Mail stop: SSOP
Washington, D.C. 20402-9328

SOME INFORMATION ON PATENTS

Should you try and get a patent for your invention? With the help of a patent attorney, Melissa Jo Buck and Elizabeth and Jeanie Low received patents for their inventions. Other inventors—such as Emma Tillman and Lauren DeLuca—are still deciding whether or not to apply for one. Many of these inventors sat down with an adult to consider the pros and cons of applying for a patent.

SOME PROS AND CONS OF APPLYING FOR A PATENT

PROS	CONS
Protects your invention	Time-consuming
Learning experience	Complicated
Allows you to sell your invention	Frustrating
Recognition for your invention	Costly (application and lawyer fees)
Feel proud	A lot of paperwork

If you're interested in applying for a patent, talk to an adult. Together, you can decide if the needed time and money are available. You'll also need to think about hiring a patent lawyer, who can help you correctly fill out the application.

A patent is an exclusive right the government grants to you so that you can prevent others from manufacturing, using, or selling an invention for a certain numbers of years. According to the U.S. Patent and Trademark Office, you can patent anything that someone can make. You can also patent the process for making something. You can't, however, patent an idea or suggestion.

To receive a patent, you must be the inventor of a product that is new and useful. You'll have to show research and drawings that prove the invention is yours. (If you've kept an Inventor's Notebook, you've already written down much of the needed information.)

When applying for a patent, you need to fulfill four requirements.

1. Provide a description of the invention, including a list of things about your invention that are unique and useful.

2. Provide a signed and notarized oath that you are the original and first inventor.

3. Provide your drawings showing how the invention is made and how it works.

4. Enclose the appropriate filing fees (basic filing fees can cost from $350 to $800).

For more information, write to the U.S. Government Printing Office and ask for the booklet titled, "General Information Concerning Patents." (The office charges a fee for this booklet.) This booklet contains a patent application and detailed information about the four requirements. Write to:

U.S. Government Printing Office
Superintendent of Documents
Mail stop: SSOP
Washington, D.C. 20402-9328

MARKETING YOUR INVENTION

Marketing means preparing your invention for sale and getting it to the people who will want to buy it: the consumers. But how do you find a company that will sell your invention? How do you know if people will buy your invention?

As with applying for a patent, talk to an adult about marketing your invention. There are many things to consider: Have you applied for or received a patent for your invention? (You'll need a patent in order to sell your invention.) Have you created a prototype of your invention? (You'll need to build a prototype to show potential companies.)

If you decide to market your invention, talk to an adult about hiring a lawyer. Although hiring a lawyer can be expensive, he or she can help you with the complex legal steps involved in selling an invention.

When planning your marketing strategy, you can either sell your invention to a manufacturer for a fee or royalty or start your own business to produce and sell your invention.

One of the nice things about selling your invention to a manufacturer is that the company will handle all the details of producing the product and getting it to the consumer. Keep in mind, though, that the manufacturer may not give you much say in decisions about your invention. Also remember that getting a manufacturer to buy your invention is no easy task.

Starting your own business is a major task that involves time, money, and risk. You can find many helpful resources about starting a business at your local library.

....

As you've read Part Two, you've seen that being an inventor requires a lot of decision-making. What materials will you use? What name will you choose? Do you apply for a patent or not? Do you market your invention or not? As an inventor, you have the opportunity to positively impact the lives of many people and to perhaps change the world. What could be more rewarding or fulfilling? Inventions are of fundamental importance to the history of civilization and the course of all human events. Whether you decide to patent and market your invention or build a working prototype, don't let your ingenuity go unused. Keep on inventing!

PART THREE

For Further Inspiration

FEMALE INVENTORS IN HISTORY

*W*HEN YOU FIND A BOOK ON INVENTORS, YOU might notice that it contains information mostly about men and their inventions. But throughout history, women, too, have solved problems and improved their lives and the lives of others with their inventions. The stories in this book prove that girls and young women can also be inventors.

In the past, laws did not exclude women from obtaining patents. But many women were afraid of what others would say if they were independent—or if they said they had invented something. Several female inventors allowed men to use their ideas and receive patents and credit for the inventions. Catherine Greene was one of these inventors. In 1792, Eli Whitney visited Greene at her Georgia plantation. Together, Greene and Whitney developed the cotton gin. Greene allowed Whitney to receive sole credit for the idea and the patent.

In the early history of the United States, most states had a law saying that a husband owned all of his wife's property. That meant a married woman was powerless to control her property or decide how it would be used or disposed of. (If a woman was single, her property was her own.)

In the early 1700s, Sybilla Masters, inventor of a corn cleaning and curing machine, applied for a patent. Because she was married, the patent was granted under her husband's name.

It wasn't until the late 1800s, when most states changed their laws, that married women were given the right to control their own property. The first woman to receive a patent in her own name was Mary Dixon Kies. The U.S. Patent and Trademark Office issued one to her in 1809 for inventing the process of weaving straw with silk or thread.

In the National Inventors Hall of Fame in Akron, Ohio, one hundred and twelve inventors have been recognized—but only three of these inventors are women. In 1991, Gertrude Elion was the first woman inducted into the Hall of Fame. Elion, who has more than forty patents in her name, invented *mercaptopurine* and several other drugs to fight diseases. In 1994, Elizabeth Hazen and Rachel Brown were also inducted. They discovered *nystatin*, the first useful anti-fungal antibiotic.

Continually through American history, the number of women receiving patents has steadily increased.

Year	Total Number of Patents	Number of Patents Issued to Women
1954	36,601	549 (1.5%)
1977	69,778	1,814 (2.6%)
1988	84,272	4,634 (5.5%)
1994	113,268	9,061 (8.0%)

SOME FEMALE INVENTORS— 3,000 B.C. TO A.D. 1994

Year	Inventor	Invention
3,000 B.C.	SeLing-She (wife of Chinese Emperor Hwang-te)	Silk cloth
380 A.D.	Hypatia of Alexandria	The Plane Astrolabe (measured the positions of the sun and stars)
1715	Sybilla Masters	Corn cleaning and curing
1772	Jane Wells	Indoor baby jumper swing
1809	Mary Dixon Kies	Weaving straw using silk or thread
1821	Sophia Woodhouse	Method of using grass, not straw, for weaving
1841	Elizabeth Adams	Corsets for pregnant women
1845	Sarah Mather	Submarine lamp and telescope
1858	Susan E. Taylor	Improved fountain pen, with a tubular ink reservoir
1860	Ellen Curtis Demorest	Home dressmaking patterns

1871	Margaret Knight	Flat-bottomed grocery-bag making machine
1873	Helen Augusta Blanchard	Sewing machine improvements
1881	Mary Walton	Elevated railway
1883	Harriett Tracy	Fire escape
1886	Josephine Cochran	Dishwashing machine
1887	Harriet Williams Strong	Dam and reservoir construction
1887	Maria Allen	Diaper
1891	Catherine Diener	Rolling pin
1896	Mary Collins	Child-carrying strap
1899	Letitia Geer	Medical syringes
1903	Mary Anderson	Windshield wiper
1904	Margaret Knight	Rotary engine
1913	Elena Mayolini DeValdes	Bottle stopper (forerunner of tamper-proof packaging)
1914	Caresse Crosby	Brassiere (first one patented)
1928	Marjorite Joyner	Permanent Wave Machine
1933	Ruth Wakefield	Chocolate chip cookie
1934	Elizabeth Kingsley	The double-crostic puzzle
1935	Eva Landman	Umbrella
1950	Bette Nesmith Graham	Liquid Paper
1954	Gertrude Elion (held 45 patents as of 1994)	Mercaptopurine and other disease-fighting drugs
1957	Elizabeth Hazen and Rachel Brown	Nystatin, anti-fungal antibiotic
1959	Ruth Handler	Barbie Doll
1969	Ann Moore and Agnes Aukerman	The Snugli child carrier
1975	Becky Schroeder	Luminescent backing sheet for writing in the dark
1976	Mary Beatrice Kenner	Carrier attachment for invalid walkers
1979	Mary Ann Moore	Pain relief composition and method of preparing the composition

1980	Mildred Kenner Smith	Family Treedition, genealogy game
1980	Valerie Thomas	Illusion Transmitter (a 3-D image that appears to be in the room with you)
1982	Alice Chatham	Space helmet, space bed
1989	Josephine Kong-Chan	Reduced-calorie and reduced-fat chocolate confectionery compositions
1991	Linda H. Dixon	Anti-snoring pillow
1992	Lori A. Cotrain	Child car-restraint garment (eliminates the need for a child car seat)
1994	Jan B. Svochak	Bifocal contact lens and method for making the lens

INSPIRING QUOTATIONS ABOUT INVENTING AND INVENTIONS

When we think of inventors, we think of people who have discovered, created, or changed something. We think of people open to learning. With those thoughts in mind, we went looking for quotations. We found some by female inventors—including some inventors you've read about in this book—as well as by other people interested in the discovering, creating, changing, and inventing process.

As you read the quotations, think about your own ideas on inventions. Look for a quotation that describes your ideas on inventing, one that you could use as a personal motto. What would you say if someone asked you for a quotation on the invention process?

"Necessity is the mother of invention."
"Don't quit five minutes before the miracle happens."
Anonymous

"Pioneers may be picturesque figures, but they are often rather lonely ones."
Nancy Astor, English politician, member of British House of Commons (1919–1945)

"Creativity comes from trust. Trust your instincts. And never hope more than you work."
Rita Mae Brown, writer, poet, and activist

"The young do not know enough to be prudent; and, therefore, they attempt the impossible—and achieve it, generation after generation."
"All things are possible until they are proved impossible."
Pearl S. Buck, novelist, 1938 Nobel Prize winner in literature

"At first people refuse to believe that a strange new thing can be done, then they begin to hope it can be done, then they see it can be done— then it is done and all the world wonders why it was not done centuries ago."
Frances Hodgson Burnett, writer

"When I can no longer create anything, I'll be done for."
Coco Chanel, French fashion designer, innovator

"Great inventors and discoverers seem to have made their discoveries and inventions as it were *by the way*, in the course of their everyday life."
Elizabeth Rundle Charles, English writer

"The only people who never fail are those who never try."
Ilka Chase, writer, actor, TV/radio personality

"I don't think necessity is the mother of invention—invention, in my opinion, arises directly from idleness, possibly also from laziness. To save oneself trouble."
Agatha Christie, English detective story writer

"Once you move beyond your fear of taking a risk, you'll realize that inventing can be really rewarding."
Kellyan Coors, inventor

"To fulfill a dream, to be allowed to sweat over lonely labor, to be given the chance to create, is the meat and potatoes of life. The money is the gravy. As everyone else, I love to dunk my crust in it. But alone, it is not a diet designed to keep body and soul together."
Bette Davis, actor

"An invention does not have to be a huge new machine or something that will change the world. An invention may be an old idea with a new twist or improvement."
Lauren Patricia DeLuca, inventor

"It is kind of fun to do the impossible."
Walt Disney, film producer

"The secret of happiness is curiosity."
Norman Douglas, English novelist, essayist

"Invention is one percent inspiration and ninety-nine percent perspiration."
Thomas Edison, inventor

"Imagination is more important than knowledge."
Albert Einstein, U.S.-Swiss-German physicist

"A problem is a chance for you to do your best."
Duke Ellington, musician

"There are at least three steps for success. First, you think that you can do it. Second, you set your mind to it. Third, you do it."
Stefanie Lynn Garry, inventor

"All acts performed in the world begin in the imagination."
Barbara Grizzuti Harrison, writer, publicist

"Great minds have purpose; others have wishes."
Washington Irving, essayist

"Remember to always think for yourself and listen to your ideas, even if they sound crazy at first."
Sarita M. James, inventor

"If one is going to change things, one has to make a fuss and catch the eye of the world."
Elizabeth Janeway, novelist, critic, essayist

"A little rebellion is a good thing."
Thomas Jefferson, president of the United States (1801–1809)

"If you want something very badly, you can achieve it. It may take patience, very hard work, a real struggle, and a long time, but it can be done."
Margo Jones, theater director

"Mistakes are the portals of discovery."
James Joyce, Irish novelist, lyric poet, playwright

"When you have an idea, go for it! Work with it, and be persistent. By inventing something, you help to make the world a better place."
Jana Kraschnewski, inventor

"The most beautiful thing in the world is, precisely, the conjunction of learning and inspiration. Oh, the passion for research and the joy of discovery!"
Wanda Landowska, Polish musician

"Innovators are inevitably controversial."
Eva Le Gallienne, actor, director, producer

"That's the way things come clear. All of a sudden. And then you realize how obvious they've been all along."
Madeleine L'Engle, writer

"That is what learning is. You suddenly understand something you've understood all your life, but in a new way."
Doris Lessing, English-Rhodesian writer, playwright

"Somewhere, something incredible is waiting to be known."
Carl Sagan, astronomer

"We don't make mistakes. We just have learnings."
Ann Wilson Schaef, psychotherapist, addictions pioneer, women's rights activist

"An important part of being a successful inventor is self-confidence."
Karen Schlangen, inventor

"Creation is everything you do. Make something."
Ntozake Shange, writer, poet, playwright

"There are no shortcuts to any place worth going."
Beverly Sills, opera singer, administrator

"When people keep telling you that you can't do a thing, you kind of like to try it."
Margaret Chase Smith, politician, member of Congress (1940–1973)

"Creations, whether they are children, poems, or organizations, take on a life of their own."
Starhawk, leader in feminine spirituality, peace activist

"Discovery consists of seeing what everybody has seen and thinking what nobody has thought."
Albert Szent-Györgyi, Hungarian-American biochemist

"Name the greatest of all the inventors: Accident."
Mark Twain, writer

"No idea is a bad idea, because it is an idea. Every idea leads to the next idea."
Jamie Lynn Villella, inventor

"Your world...you have created it for yourself, it is real to yourself, and therefore real to us.... It is for you to discover yourself in a world where, alone and free, you may dream the possible dream: that the wondrous is real, because that is how you feel it to be, how you wish it to be...and how you wish it into being."
Diana Vreeland, fashion editor/journalist

"Do not let what you cannot do interfere with what you can do."
John Wooden, basketball coach

ORGANIZATIONS AND ASSOCIATIONS TO CONTACT

Where can you get more information about inventing? In this section, you'll learn about many places that provide information on topics regarding inventions. To help inventors, a few of these groups produce newsletters; others print information about their services. Some give technical assistance, while others sponsor meetings, seminars, conferences, and competitions.

Almost every state has statewide, regional, or local associations for people interested in the inventing process. These associations may provide printed information and sponsor meetings. Look for listings in the phone directory of the capital city in your state or in your local directory. Joining an association is a great way to learn more about inventing. You can also share your ideas with others who have similar interests and abilities.

When you contact an organization, ask for information about its services and resources. Ask about membership and service fees. What will you receive for your money? Ask if the organization is an *invention marketer* or *invention broker*. An invention marketer finds businesses that will sell an inventor's product. An invention broker negotiates contracts between an inventor and a manufacturing company. Both marketers and brokers charge fees or receive commissions from the invention's profits.

If you write a letter to an organization, include a self-addressed stamped envelope. Once you receive the information, read through it carefully with an adult. *Never* send an invention or idea to an organization before first checking it out.

The American Society of Inventors, Incorporated (ASI)
P.O. Box 58426
Philadelphia, PA 19102
Telephone: (215) 546-6601

The ASI is an independent, nonprofit organization that provides its members with technical, legal, and business information to support their inventive efforts. It provides general public information regarding the inventive process. Members receive a bi-monthly ASI newsletter, *American Heritage of Invention and Technology* (free subscription), ASI recommended information index, and an ASI Inventors Notebook. ASI charges an annual membership fee. Two forms of membership are available: introductory and full membership.

Duracell/NSTA Scholarship Competition
National Science Teachers Association
1840 Wilson Boulevard
Arlington, VA 22201-3000

Duracell USA sponsors this annual competition, which the National Science Teachers Association (NSTA) administers. The competition is open to all students in grades 9 through 12. The contest requires that inventions be working devices, powered by Duracell batteries and performing a practical function. Entries are limited to those created by one inventor alone, not pairs or groups. The competition awards U.S. savings bonds of up to $20,000.

Innovation Institute
901 South National Avenue, Box 88
Springfield, MO 65804-0089
Telephone: (417) 836-5072
    The Innovation Institute and The College of Business Administration at Southwest Missouri State University are part of the Wal-Mart Innovation Network (WIN) program. These groups provide an evaluation service, which provides inventors with an honest and objective analysis of the risks and potential of their ideas and inventions. The groups' primary objective is to stimulate new job opportunities for Americans by keeping American ingenuity in the United States. There are no publications or membership fees.

Intellectual Property Owners (IPO)
1255 Twenty-Third Street, N.W, Suite 850
Washington, DC 20037
Telephone: (202) 466-2396; FAX: (202) 466-2893
    IPO is a nonprofit association representing people who own patents, trademarks, copyrights, and trade secrets. This group sponsors awards such as the Spirit of American Ingenuity Award and The National Inventor of the Year Award. IPO publishes the *IPO Washington Brief*, which is faxed or mailed to all members twice a month, and *IPO News and Analysis*, a quarterly newsletter for members. Annual meetings are held. IPO charges a membership fee for individuals and inventors' groups. Included in the membership are publications, committee memberships, and discounted entrance and registration fees for IPO meetings and conferences.

Invent America!
U.S. Patent Model Foundation
1505 Powhatan Street
Alexandria, VA 22314
Telephone: (703) 684-1836

This organization sponsors the Invent America! Competitions in elementary and middle schools across the United States. It provides state, regional, and national level awards for students' inventions that solve everyday problems. This group also provides educational materials, teacher training and recognition, and annual awards for students. Charges a fee for their information packet.

Inventors Workshop International Education Foundation (IWIEF)
1029 Castillo Street
Santa Barbara, CA 93101-3736
Telephone: (805) 962-5722

This group sponsors "The Great Idea Contest," an annual competition for student inventors of all ages. IWIEF publishes several periodicals geared to specific age groups of inventors. Discounted membership fees for students.

Inventure Place
221 South Broadway Street
Akron, OH 44308
Telephone: (216) 762-4463; FAX: (216) 762-6313
Speakline 1-800-993-8000

Inventure Place is the first institution of its kind to combine a natural resource center for creativity, educational outreach, and curriculum development programs for schools and businesses. It offers the Inventors Workshop and sponsors the National Inventors Hall of Fame. Its goal is to become a national center of education and creativity dedicated to inspiring invention in people of many different educational levels and styles of learning. Programs offered are Camp Invention (grades 1–6), Camp Ingenuity (grades 7–9), and the BF Goodrich Collegiate Inventors Program. Quarterly newsletters.

National Inventive Thinking Association (NITA)
Living Resource Center
Houston Independent School District
11833 Chimney Rock
Houston, TX 77035

NITA is a nonprofit organization of educators, business leaders, and government representatives. It provides its members with consultants at the K–12 and college/university level and is a clearinghouse for instructional materials from across the country. The group also sponsors a speakers' bureau and provides advice and assistance from intellectual property law associations and various creativity centers. It also offers activities sponsored by the U.S. Patent and Trademark Office. NITA hosts an annual conference on creative and thinking skills for children to help develop and apply critical and creative thinking and problem-solving skills. Membership is offered to people who pay a fee and register for the annual conference.

Project XL
Administrator
U.S. Patent and Trademark Office
Washington, DC 20231
Telephone: (703) 557-1610

Sponsored by many different inventors' and government organizations, Project XL is an outreach program that encourages the development of inventive thinking and problem-solving skills.

Silver Burdett & Ginn
250 James Street
Morristown, NJ 07960
Telephone: (201) 285-7740

This textbook publishing company sponsors the SBG Invention Convention for grades 1 through 9. Individual schools hold the competitions, and their winners are eligible for the International Invention Convention. The company provides materials free of charge to purchasers of their textbooks.

U.S. Department of Commerce
Office of Patents and Trademarks
Washington, DC 20231
Telephone: (703) 308-HELP (703-308-4357)

This is the government agency that evaluates, grants, and holds records on all registered U.S. Patents. It provides information on how to obtain patents or trademarks. It also lists attorneys and agents who have met the legal, scientific, and technical requirements of the patent office and have agreed to uphold professional standards of conduct.

U.S. Department of Energy
Washington, DC 20585

This office oversees the Energy Related Inventions Program, established in 1975. The government helps individuals and small company inventors develop their non-nuclear energy technologies. The office evaluates invention disclosures on the basis of technical feasibility, energy conservation or supply potential, and commercial possibilities. The office forwards promising inventions to the Department of Energy for possible financial support. This department conducts two-day seminars at various locations across the United States. The seminars cover topics such as patenting and protection, estimating the worth of your invention, licensing, marketing, new business start-up, research and development, and venture financing.

BOOKS TO READ

In this book, you've found out where some inventors got their ideas and what steps they took to change their ideas into inventions. You've read about what has motivated people to become inventors and how some have continued with the inventing process for many years. You can find out more about inventors and the inventing process by reading other books.

Look over the titles listed in this section and decide on the ones you'll want to read now and those you may want to read later. To help you in your search, we've listed books for elementary school readers followed by books for young adult readers.

Your school or community library may have copies of these books. If you don't find them, ask a librarian. The librarian may order a particular book for you—or find one on a similar subject. Look for other books and start your own reading list to share with your friends, teachers, and family. Enjoy reading about inventors and inventing—it's fun and you'll learn new things about others and, possibly, about yourself as well!

BOOKS FOR ELEMENTARY GRADES

Andrews and McMeel, *Flintstones Wacky Inventions: How Things Work in the Modern World* (Atlanta, Georgia: Turner, 1993).

Bendick, J., *Eureka! It's a Telephone!* (Brookfield, Connecticut: Millbrook, 1993).

Brown, J., and M. Hott, *Inventing Things* (Milwaukee, Wisconsin: Gareth Stevens, 1990).

Brubaker, .E.A., and D.R. Garmire, *Inventing for Kids* (East Windsor Hill, Connecticut: Synergetics, 1992).

Clements, G., *The Picture History of Great Inventors* (New York: Knopf Books for Young Readers, 1994).

Conley, K., *Benjamin Banneker: Scientist and Mathematician* (Broomall, Pennsylvania: Chelsea House, 1989).

Cranford, G., *Albert Schweitzer* (Columbus, Ohio: Silver Burdett Press, 1990).

Curson, M., *Jonas Salk* (Columbus, Ohio: Silver Burdett Press, 1990).

Farley, K.C., *Robert H. Goddard* (Columbus, Ohio: Silver Burdett Press, 1990).

Gardner, R., *Experimenting with Inventions* (New York: Watts, Franklin, 1990).

Gray, J.M., *George Washington Carver* (Columbus, Ohio: Silver Burdett Press, 1990).

Groves, S., and D.D. Buchman, *What If? Fifty Discoveries That Changed the World* (New York: Scholastic, 1988).

Hargrove, Jim, *Dr. An Wang: Computer Pioneer* (Chicago: Children's Press, 1993).

Haynes, R.M., *The Wright Brothers* (Columbus, Ohio: Silver Burdett Press, 1990).

Holmes, B., *George Eastman* (Columbus, Ohio: Silver Burdett Press, 1990).

Igpen, R., and P. Wilkinson, *Ideas That Changed the World: The Greatest Discoveries and Inventions* (Broomall, Pennsylvania: Chelsea House, 1994).

Inventive Genius (Columbus, Ohio: Silver Burdett Press, 1993).

Ireland, K., *Albert Einstein* (Columbus, Ohio: Silver Burdett Press, 1990).

Jacobs, D., *What Does It Do?: Inventions Then and Now* (Chatham, New Jersey: Raintree Steck-Vaughn Publishers, 1990).

James, P., *The Real McCoy: African-American Invention and Innovation, 1619–1930* (Washington, D.C.: Smithsonian Institution Press, 1989).

Jones, C.F., *Mistakes That Worked* (New York: Doubleday, 1991).

Kerby, M., *Samuel Morse* (New York: Franklin Watts, 1991).

Konigsburg, E.L., *Samuel Todd's Book of Great Inventions* (New York: Macmillan Children's Book Group, 1991).

Lomask, M., *Great Lives: Invention and Technology* (New York: Macmillan Children's Book Group, 1991).

Macaulay, D., *The Way Things Work* (Boston: Houghton Mifflin, 1988).

Machines and Inventions (Alexandria, Virginia: Time-Life, 1993).

Montgomery, M., *Marie Curie* (Morristown, New Jersey: Good Apple, 1990).

Nicholson, L.P., *George Washington Carver* (Broomall, Pennsylvania: Chelsea House, 1994).

Parker, S., *Guglielmo Marconi and Radio* (Broomall, Pennsylvania: Chelsea House, 1994).

Patton, S. and M. Maletis, *Inventors* (Tucson, Arizona: Zephyr Press, 1989).

Pelta, K., *Alexander Graham Bell* (Columbus, Ohio: Silver Burdett Press, 1989).

Peterson, P.R., *The Know It All: Resource Book for Kids* (Tucson, Arizona: Zephyr Press, 1989).

Potter, R.R., *Benjamin Franklin* (Columbus, Ohio: Silver Burdett Press, 1990).

————, *Buckminster Fuller* (Columbus, Ohio: Silver Burdett Press, 1990).

Richardson, R.O., *The Weird and Wondrous World of Patents* (New York: Sterling, 1990).

Stanish, B., *The Ambidextrous Mind* (Morristown, New Jersey: Good Apple, 1989).

Swanson, J., *David Bushnell and His Turtle: The Story of America's First Submarine* (New York: Macmillan Children's Book Group, 1991).

Sylvester, D., *Inventions* (Santa Barbara, California: Learning Works, 1992).

Tanner, J., *Futuristics: A Time to Come* (Tucson, Arizona: Zephyr Press, 1992).

Turvey, P., *Inventions: Inventors and Ingenious Ideas* (New York: Franklin Watts, 1992).

BOOKS FOR YOUNG ADULTS AND UP

Arner, B., *Invent* (Lakeside, California: Interact, 1994).

Bender, L., *Invention* (New York: Knopf Books for Young Readers, 1991).

Brophy, A., *John Ericson and the Inventions of War* (Columbus, Ohio: Silver Burdett Press, 1990).

Filson, B., *Superconductors and Other New Breakthroughs in Science* (New York: Simon and Schuster, 1989).

Flack, J.D., *Inventing, Inventions, and Inventors: A Handbook for Teachers of the Gifted and Talented* (Englewood, Colorado: Libraries Unlimited, 1989).

Griffin, L., and K. McCann, *The Book of Women: 300 Notable Women History Passed By* (Holbrook, Massachusetts: Bob Adams, 1992).

Haskins, J., *Outward Dreams: Black Inventors and Their Inventions* (New York: Walker and Company, 1991).

Historical Inventions on File (New York: Facts on File, 1994).

Inventors and Inventions (Phoenix: Engine-Unity, 1988).

Klein, D., *The Inventive Process* (Palo Alto, California: Dale Seymour Publications, 1990).

Lafferty, P., and J. Rowe, *The Inventor through History* (New York: Thomson Learning, 1993).

Lambert, D., and T. Osmond, *Great Discoveries and Inventions* (New York: Facts on File, 1988).

Lehman, J., *Invendex, Inventors Index, Sparks the Flash of Genius* (Sheboygan, Wisconsin: WLC Publishing, 1993).

MacDonald, A., *Feminine Ingenuity: Women and Invention in America* (New York: Ballantine, 1992).

Markham, L., *Inventions That Changed Modern Life* (Chatham, New Jersey: Raintree Steck-Vaughn Publishers, 1993).

McPartland, S., *Edwin Land* (Vero Beach, Florida: Rourke Enterprises, 1993).

Noonan, G. J., *Nineteenth-Century Inventors* (New York: Facts on File, 1992).

Olsen, F. H., *Inventors Who Left Their Brand on America* (New York: Bantam Books, 1991).

Prostano, E., *Take Two Inventions and Two Patents* (Stuart, Florida: In-Time Publications, 1991).

Reid, S., *Inventions and Trade* (New York: Macmillan, 1994).

Reid, S., and P. Fara, *The Usborne Book of Discovery* (London: Usborne Publishing Limited, 1994).
———, *The Usborne Book of Inventors* (London: Usborne Publishing Limited, 1994).

Stanley, A., *Mothers and Daughters of Invention: A Revised History of Technology* (Metuchen, New Jersey: Scarecrow Press, 1993).

Taylor, B., *Charles Ginsburg* (Vero Beach, Florida: Rourke Enterprises, 1993).

Travers, B., *World of Invention* (Detroit, Michigan: Gale Research, 1993).

Van Steenwyk, E., *Levi Strauss: The Blue Jeans Man* (New York: Walker and Company, 1988).

Williams, B., *Karl Benz* (New York: Franklin Watts, 1991).

Yount, L., *Black Scientists* (New York: Facts on File, 1991).

Index

A

Acceptance-finding, 133, 134
Acronyms, 135
Adjustable broom, 131
Alarms
    bathtub, 120
    cabinet, 47–48
Aluminum on fire, 62
American Heritage of Invention and Technology (ASI newsletter), 152
American Society of Inventors, Incorporated (ASI), 152
Arthritis Foundation, 48
Arthritis, inventions for, 48, 120, 130
ASI. *See* American Society of Inventors, Incorporated (ASI)
Associations and organizations, to contact, 2, 151–156
Asthmameter, 93, 95–98, *96, 98,* 132
Astor, Nancy, 147

B

BF Goodrich Collegiate Inventors Program, 155
Baby wipes, in diaper, 15
Bar codes. *See* Scanner
Bathtub alarm. *See under* Alarms
Bean, Suzanne, 168
Blind finder, 95
Books to read, 2
    for elementary grades, 157–160
    for young adults, 160–161

"Boys, Scoot Over! Girls, Advance to the Top!" (game), 71–73
Broom, adjustable, 32–36, *34, 36*
Brown, Rachel, 144, 145
Brown, Rita Mae, 147
Buck, Melissa Jo, 26–31, *27, 28,* 130, 137
Buck, Pearl S., 147
Burnett, Frances Hodgson, 147

C

Cabinet alarm. *See under* Alarms
Camp Ingenuity, 155
Camp Invention, 154–155
Chairs, tipping backwards, 106–107. *See also* Stools
Chanel, Coco, 147
Charles, Elizabeth Rundle, 147
Chase, Ilka, 147
Christie, Agatha, 147
Clip-tack, 47
Clothes saver, 37–40, *39,* 134
Computers
    on helicopters, 112
    for patent searches, 84–85
    and speech recognition, 111–115
Conservation inventions, 53–64
    questions and ideas, 64
Convenience inventions, 5–24
    questions and ideas, 24
Coors, Kellyan, 66–74, *68, 71,* 148
Copy machine. *See* Photocopy machine
Cotton gin, 143

162

D

Davis, Bette, 148
Decision-making, 132–133, 139
DeLuca, Lauren Patricia, 88–92, *89, 91*, 137, 148
Desk pocket, 30
Diapers, 14–18, *16*
Disney, Walt, 148
Dolls, Barbie, 145
Donabar, Jennifer, 6–9, *7, 8*
Doorknobs, cushioned, 120
Doormat, circular with spinning brushes, 120
Douglas, Norman, 148
Drawing, of invention, 134
Driver's license, number scanner, 54–57, *56*, 131
Duracell/NSTA Scholarship Competition, 152–153

E

E.Z. Tools, 48–49, 130
Edison, Thomas, 148
    laboratory, 102
Einstein, Albert, 148
Electronic lock. *See* Lock, electronic
Electronic Neighborhood Watch, 49–50
Elementary students, books for, 157–160
Elion, Gertrude, 144, 145
Ellington, Duke, 148
Energy Related Inventions Program, 156

F

Fact-finding, 131
Feeder-keeper, 93–94
Female inventors. *See* Women inventors

Ford (Henry) Museum. *See* Henry Ford Museum
Freudenstein, Ferdinand, 19
Fun inventions, 65–86
    questions and ideas, 86

G

Garcia, Jennifer, 10–13, *11, 12*, 135
Garry, Stefanie Lynn, 32–26, *33, 34*, 131, 148
Girls and Young Women Leading the Way (Karnes & Bean), 168
Girls, gifted, game for, 70–73, *71*
Gloves, sand-filled, 75–80, *80*
Great Idea Contest, 154
Greene, Catherine, 143
Greenfield Village (Dearborn, Mich.), 44

H

Hair bow holder, 94
Hall of Fame. *See* National Inventors Hall of Fame
Hamster breeding, 74
Happy Hands, 75–80, *80*
Harfmann, Katya, 106–110, *107, 109*, 134
Harrison, Barbara Grizzuti, 149
Hat, hide-away, 47
Hatfield, Meghan Renee, 54–57, *55*, 131
Hazen, Elizabeth, 144, 145
Health inventions, 87–104, 144
    questions and ideas, 104
Hearing, 69
Helicopters, computers, 112
Henry Ford Museum (Dearborn, Mich.), 44

High school students, books for,
160–161
Houston Inventors Association, 77

I

Ice blades, 81–85, *84*, 135
Ice cream scooper, 18
Ideas
    coming up with, 128–129
    finding, 132
    pursuing, 130
    survey for gathering, 129
    turning into inventions, 131
Incubation time, 131
In-line skating, 81–85
Innovation Institute, 153
Innovations, 102
INPEX. *See* Inventing New Products
    Exposition (INPEX)
Inspiration, resources for, 2, 141–161
Intellectual Property Owners (IPO),
153
International Invention Convention,
156
International Science and Engineering
    Fair, Annual, 114
Invent America! competitions, 154
    asthmameter, 98
    broom, 33, 35
    clothes saver, 38, 40
    driver's license number scanner,
      55–56
    electronic lock, 6
    gifted girls game, 71, 72–73
    ice blades, 85
    meal markers, 90
    nebuwhirl, 99, 100, 102
    pocket diaper, 17
    stalk board, 60
    swimming pool cover, 43–44
    tipper toes, 108–109

    vacuum dirt mat, 10, 12
Inventing and inventions
    benefits of, 127
    defined, 91
    choosing an idea, 130
    coming up with ideas, 128–129
    getting started, 127–128
    successful, 120–121
    See also Inventors
Inventing New Products Exposition
    (INPEX), 119–120
Invention brokers, 152
Invention marketers, 152
Inventors
    how to be one, 2, 125–139
    resources for, 2, 141–161
    tips for, 57, 63
Inventor's clubs, 86, 118
Inventor's Digest magazine, 78, 119
Inventor's notebook, 2
    drawings and sketches, 134
    fact-finding, 131
    getting started, 127–128
    ideas, 128–129, 130, 131
    as log, 90
    names, ideas for, 135, 136
    patent applications, requirements,
      138
    plans, 133
    problem-finding, 132
Inventors Workshop, 154
Inventors Workshop International
    Education Foundation (IWIEF),
    154
Inventure Place, 154
IPO. *See* Intellectual Property Owners
    (IPO)
IPO News and Analysis (newsletter),
153
Irving, Washington, 149

IWIEF. *See* Inventors Workshop International Education Foundation (IWIEF)

J

James, Sarita M., 111–115, *113, 114,* 149
Janeway, Elizabeth, 149
Jefferson, Thomas, 149
"Jenny Jones" (TV show), 17
Jones, Margo, 149
Joyce, James, 149

K

Karnes, Frances, 168
Kiddie stool. *See* Stools
Kids R Us magazine, 78
Kies, Mary Dixon, 143, 144
Kraschnewski, Jana, 58–63, *59,* 149

L

Landowska, Wanda, 149
Lanmon, Chelsea, 14–18, *15, 16*
Laundry. *See* Clothes saver
Le Gallienne, Eva, 149
Lee, Jeri, 93–98, *94, 96,* 132
L'Engle, Madeleine, 150
Lens, doctor's, 79
Lessing, Doris, 150
Light, tooth fairy, 67–68
Lock, electronic, 6–9
Low, Elizabeth, 75–80, *76, 79,* 116, 119, 120, 137
Low, Jeanie, 78–79, 116–122, *117, 118,* 137

M

Macaulay, David, 55, 96, 104, 159
Marketing inventions, 138–139
Masters, Sybilla, 143, 144
Mattress cover, flame-resistant, 79
Meal markers, 88–92, *91, 92*
Medical inventions. *See* Health inventions
Mercaptopurine, 144
Models
    of inventions, 134–135
    meal markers, 89–90
    tipper toes, 107–108
    See also Prototypes
Mop head cover, 26–31, *28, 31*

N

Names of inventions, 135–136. *See also* Trademarks
National Inventive Thinking Association (NITA), 155
National Inventor of the Year Award, 153
National Inventors Hall of Fame, 143–144, 154
National Science Teachers Association (NSTA), 152–153
Nebulizers, 99–100
Nebuwhirl, 99–103, *102, 103,* 130
Neubauer, Laura, 99–103, *100, 102,* 130
Neural networks, 112, 113
Nintendo Kids' Platform, 45
NITA. *See* National Inventive Thinking Association (NITA)
Nobel Prize, 114–115
Noise control, 69–70

NSTA. *See* National Science Teachers Association (NSTA)
Nystatin, 144

O

"The Oprah Winfrey Show" (TV show), 17
Organizations and associations, to contact, 2, 151–156
Osborn, Alex, 131

P

Parnes, Sidney, 131
Patent and Trademark Depository Libraries (PTDLs), 136
Patents, 137–138
    applying for, 137–138
    computer searches, 84–85
    defined, 137
    issued to women, 144
Phonemes, 113
Photocopy machine, erasing, 13
Pocket, desk, 30
Pocket diaper, 14–18, *16*
Problem-finding, 132
Problem-solving
    creative process, 131
    health inventions, 92, 93, 98, 102
    ideas for inventions, 130
    safety inventions, 106, 115, 120
Project XL, 155
Prototypes
    building, 135
    defined, 135
    ice blades, 82–83, 135
    See also Models
PTDLs. *See* Patent and Trademark Depository Libraries (PTDLs)

Q

Quotations, about inventing and inventions, 2, 146–151

R

Roller blades, 81–85

S

Safety inventions, 105–123
    questions and ideas, 123
Sagan, Carl, 150
Sayegh, Samir, Dr., 112
SBG Invention Convention, 156
Scanner, driver's license, 54–57, *56*, 131
Schaef, Ann Wilson, 150
Schlangen, Karen, 19–23, *20, 22,* 150
Science fairs, 112
Scissors, 19–20
Selling inventions. *See* Marketing inventions
Shange, Ntozake, 150
SHHHH machine, 69–70
Shoe, grow-a-size, 47
Shovel, E.Z., 48
Sills, Beverly, 150
Silver Burdett & Ginn, 156
Skating. *See* Ice blades; In-line skating
Sketch development, 134
Sleeve smoother, 17
Smith, Margaret Chase, 150
Smoke sensor, 18
Solution-finding, 132–133. *See also* Decision-making
South African Invention Society, 79

Speech recognition, and computers, 111–115
Spirit of American Ingenuity Award, 153
Splash guard, 94
Stalk board, 58–63, *61*
Starhawk, 150
Stewart, Katina, 37–40, *38, 39*, 134
Stools
    kiddie stool, 116–122, *118, 122*
    step-stools, 116
    See also Chairs
STRETCH, 26, 29
Supplementary Teaching Resources for Educationally Talented Children (STRETCH), 26, 29
Swimming pool cover, 41–44, *44*
Szent-Györgyi, Albert, 150

Tillman, Emma, 41–44, *43, 44*, 130, 137
Timelines, 133
Tipper toes, 106–110, *109, 110*, 134
Tools, E.Z., 48–49, 130
Trademarks, registering, 136
Tri-City Inventor's Fair, 50
Tucker, Emily Meredith, 81–85, *82, 84*, 135
Twain, Mark, 151

Umbrella, 19–23, *22, 23*
Uncopy machine, 13
U.S. Department of Commerce, Office of Patents and Trademarks, 156
U.S. Department of Energy, 156

U.S. Government Printing Office, Superintendent of Documents, 136, 138
U.S. Patent and Trademark Office, 137, 155
U.S. Patent Model Foundation, 154
USA Inventors Exposition, 79

Vacuum cleaners, 48–49, 130
    dirt mat, 10–13, *12*, 135
Viars, Jan, 114
Villella, Jamie Lynn, 45–50, *46, 48*, 130, 151
Visually impaired, inventions for, 95
Vreeland, Diana, 151

W

Wal-Mart Innovation Network (WIN) program, 153
Washington Brief (IPO), 153
The Washington Post, 79
Wavelets, 112
The Way Things Work (Macaulay), 55, 96, 104, 159
Whitney, Eli, 143
"Why Didn't I Think of That?" (TV show), 78
WIN. *See* Wal-Mart Innovation Network (WIN) program
Women inventors, in history, 143–146
Women's Day magazine, 78
Wooden, John, 151
Work-saving inventions, 25–51
    questions and ideas, 51

Y

Young adults, books for, 160–161

About the Authors

$\mathcal{F}$rances Karnes received her Ph.D. in Education from the University of Illinois. She is currently Professor of Special Education at the University of Southern Mississippi, and has been part of the university faculty for over two decades. She is Director of The Center for Gifted Studies and the center's Director of the Leadership Studies Program for grades 6–11. A course on inventing is offered through the Summer Gifted Studies Program for grades 4–8.

Frances is a past president of The Association for the Gifted, a national organization, and the founder and first president of the Mississippi Association for the Gifted. She has co-authored nine books and over one hundred and thirty journal articles on a variety of subjects including leadership, gifted children, and legal issues. Frances resides in Hattiesburg, Mississippi, with her husband, Dr. M. Ray Karnes. Family members are Christopher, John, Leighanne, and Mary Ryan Karnes.

Suzanne Bean received her B.S. in Elementary Education from Delta State University in Mississippi and earned her M.Ed. and Ph.D. in Special Education (with an emphasis in Gifted Education) from the University of Southern Mississippi. She is currently an associate professor of education at the Mississippi University for Women in Columbus. She is also Director of the Mississippi Governor's School, a residential program for high school students who show high intellectual, creative, and leadership potential. She was recently elected Vice Chair of the National Conference on Governor's Schools.

Suzanne has served as President of the Mississippi Association of Talented and Gifted and has participated in numerous conference and workshop presentations. She is also a consultant in the area of education of the gifted. Suzanne and her husband, Dr. Mark H. Bean, have two children, a daughter, Cameron Meriweather, and a son, Mark Hudson.

The first book Frances and Suzanne wrote together, *Girls and Young Women Leading the Way*, was published in 1993 by Free Spirit Publishing.

More Books from Free Spirit

Girls and Young Women Leading the Way:
20 True Stories about Leadership
by Frances A. Karnes, Ph.D.,
and Suzanne M. Bean, Ph.D.

The Young Person's Guide to Becoming a Writer
by Janet E. Grant

The Kid's Guide to Service Projects:
Over 500 Service Ideas for Young People
Who Want to Make a Difference
by Barbara A. Lewis

Fighting Invisible Tigers:
A Stress Management Guide for Teens
by Earl Hipp

Psychology for Kids II:
40 Fun Experiments That Help You Learn About Others
by Jonni Kincher

Becoming Myself:
True Stories about Learning from Life
by Cassandra Walker Simmons

Making the Most of Today:
Daily Readings for Young People on Self-Awareness,
Creativity, and Self-Esteem
by Pamela Espeland and Rosemary Wallner

To place an order, or to request a free catalog of
SELF-HELP FOR KIDS® materials, write or call:

Free Spirit Publishing Inc.
400 First Avenue North, Suite 616
Minneapolis, MN 55401-1730
toll-free (800) 735-7323
local (612) 338-2068